Mark Water

CHRISTIAN LIVING

made simple

AMG
Publishers

God's Word is our highest calling.

AMG Publishers
6815 Shallowford Road
Chattanooga, Tennessee 37421

Copyright © 2002 John Hunt Publishing Ltd
Text © 2002 Mark Water

ISBN 0-89957-429-7

Designed by Andrew Milne Design

Printed in China.

'Picture Acknowledgement:
P121 'The Light of the World'. By permission of the
Warden and Fellows of Keble College, Oxford.

Contents

How to grow

All Christians long to know how they can be the Christians God intended them to be. This volume explains how this can be achieved. Through a series of Bible studies you will discover how to start the Christian life, how to grow in the Christian life, and how to overcome problems in the Christian life.

You may have wondered why so many Christians collapse, and why, out of the many students who swell the ranks of university Christian groups, only a minority are active members of any Christian fellowship by the time they are forty. This serious problem is also addressed.

Becoming a spiritually mature Christian is a most worthwhile end in itself. But this volume also looks beyond questions of your own relationship with God to show you how you can share your faith with non-Christians and how you can be an effective counselor to fellow-Christians.

When Billy Graham was at the height of his powers, leading evangelistic crusades throughout the world, he once remarked, "One of my great regrets is that I have not studied enough. I wish I had studied more and preached less." It is hoped that *Christian Living Made Simple* may be an encouragement to Christians to study the Bible more.

1   STARTING THE CHRISTIAN LIFE

CONTENTS	
	page
INTRODUCTION	6
ISN'T EVERYONE A CHILD OF GOD?	8-9
WHAT IS A "BORN-AGAIN" CHRISTIAN?	10-11
HOW CAN I BE SURE THAT I'M A CHRISTIAN?	12-15

Introduction

Jesus was the greatest personal evangelist the world has ever seen. To understand the meaning of being "born again" we have to observe and study his life and conversations. The Bible study on John chapter 4 shows how Jesus led the Samaritan woman from her world of darkness into the light. The study on John chapter 3 shows how Jesus took a totally different approach with a leading rabbi. As Os Guinness has observed, "Christ is the only way to God, but there are as many ways to Christ as there are people who come to him."

Countless Christians are plagued with doubts about their own Christian life and wonder if they are Christians at all. Bible studies based on John's first letter, which appears to have been written as a "follow-up" letter to new Christians, focus on John's teaching on how we can be certain about our faith.

We need to understand this for, to quote Billy Graham again, "The devil will do everything in his power to sow seeds of doubt in your mind as to whether your conversion is a reality or not."

Isn't everyone a child of God?

True or false?

It would be nice if everyone was a child of God. Of course everyone is ultimately created by the Creator of the universe, whether they acknowledge it or not. But the Bible teaches that everyone is not a child of God.

Take the example of Jesus

If anyone was God's child you'd have thought that it would have been the top religious leaders of Jesus' day. However, some of Jesus' most severe words ever recorded were directed at the teachers of the law and Pharisees. Jesus told them to their faces that they were:

- **blind guides**, Matthew 23:16
- **blind fools**, Matthew 23:17
- **hypocrites**, Matthew 23:25
- **whitewashed tombs**, which look beautiful on the outside but on the inside are full of dead men's bones and everything unclean, Matthew 23:27
- **snakes! brood of vipers!** Matthew 23:33

There is not much here about these people being God's children! Jesus even asked them, "How will you escape being condemned to hell?" Matthew 23:33

Jesus caused divisions

It is true large crowds of people listened to Jesus with delight, Mark 12:37. However, not everyone who spoke to Jesus had a happy encounter. The description of the rich young man leaving Jesus is one of the saddest verses in the New Testament: "When the young man heard this, he went away sad, because he had great wealth" Matthew 19:22.

Even a superficial reading of the four Gospels shows how at the end of Jesus teaching the crowds there was a division. Some believed in Jesus, others did not believe. After Jesus raised Lazarus from the dead there were some Jews present who "put their faith in him," John 11:45. But there were other Jews who reported this event to the Pharisees, and as a result, "from that day on they plotted to take his life," John 11:53.

Different concepts but the same basic meaning

The New Testament teaches that nobody is born Christian, but rather that everyone must become a Christian. There are many different words and concepts used in the New Testament to describe a Christian. From just a cursory study of these different words it is obvious that becoming a Christian is a momentous step.

A Christian is someone who has:

- moved from darkness into light: 1 Peter 2:9
- moved from death into life: John 5:24
- received the gift of eternal life: Romans 6:23.

A Christian is someone who is:

- a brother or sister of Jesus: Matthew 12:48-50
- a follower of Jesus: Luke 14:27
- a friend of Jesus: John 15:15
- a believer in Jesus: John 4:41
- a disciple of Jesus: John 8:31.

Children of the devil

Jesus taught that his heavenly Father causes the sun to shine on the good and the evil and that he sends his rain on the righteous and on the unrighteous, Matthew 5:45. In that very general sense we may say that God sends his blessings on everyone. But Jesus never taught that everyone is a child of God. Rather, he taught that some people were even children of the devil. Jesus said to some Jews that if God was really their Father they would love him [that is, love Jesus] because he came from God the Father. He went on to say to them: "You belong to your father, the devil, and you want to carry out your father's desire" John 8:44.

Heaven and hell

If everyone was a child of God just because they have been born physically, there would be no need for any heaven and hell. There would only be heaven. Yet the person who spoke most about heaven and hell in the New Testament was Jesus. See Matthew 5:22, 29, 30; 10:28; 18:9; 23;15, 33. Mark 9:43, 45, 47; Luke 12:5; 16:23.

Jesus told his disciples, "Do not be afraid of those who kill the body...Fear him who, after the killing of the body, has power to throw you into hell" Luke 12:4, 5.

What is a "born-again" Christian?

Defining a Christian
In every generation Christians have believed that, "The most important single thing you can do in your life is to establish a personal relationship with Jesus Christ, in which he is your personal Lord and Savior, and you are his trusting follower."

Why talk about "born-again" Christians?
A national survey taken at the turn of the millennium found that about 50% of the American population claimed to be "born-again Christians." It's a pity that it should ever have been necessary to qualify the word "Christian." For all Christians should be "born-again" Christians. It is not possible to be a Christian without being born again.

In the early days of the church Barnabas and Saul [Paul] spent a year teaching large numbers of people in Antioch about Christianity. As a result, "The disciples were called Christians first at Antioch," Acts 11:26. They were not called "born-again" Christians, just "Christians."

Nicodemus
If you want information about "born-again" Christians the place to look is John chapter 3:1-15. There, thanks to the night-time visit of a leading Jewish Pharisee, Nicodemus, to Jesus, we have Jesus' teaching on this subject.

Jesus told his visitor, "I tell you the truth, no one can see the kingdom of God unless he is born again," John 3:3.

From this conversation there is no getting away from the fact that the new birth is a necessity.

Defining this new birth
What this new birth is not
The new birth is not achieved by doing good things. "He saved us, not because of the righteous things we had done" Titus 3:5.

What this new birth is
The new birth is **a rebirth and renewal** by the Holy Spirit."He saved us through the washing of rebirth and renewal…" Titus 3:5. The new birth is **sharing in God's life**. "So that…you may participate in the divine nature" 2 Peter 1:4.

The new birth **moves us** from the kingdom of darkness **into the kingdom of light**. "For he has rescued us from the dominion of darkness and brought us into the kingdom of the Son he loves" Colossians 1:13.

The new birth is **a spiritual creation**. "Therefore, if anyone is in Christ, he is a new creation; the old has gone, the new has come!" 2 Corinthians 5:17.

The necessity of the new birth
The condition of humankind makes it necessary. "For all have sinned and fall short of the glory of God" Romans 3:23.

Nobody can make himself or herself holy. "Can the Ethiopian change his skin or the leopard its spots? Neither can you do good who are accustomed to doing evil" Jeremiah 13:23.

Jesus said that the new birth was necessary. [Note the "must" in the following verse.] "You must be born again" John 3:7.

God's holiness makes the new birth a necessity. "Make every effort…to be holy; without holiness no one will see the Lord" Hebrews 12:14.

How new birth is given
It is God's work and is given by the Holy Spirit through Jesus. "He saved us…by the Holy Spirit, whom he poured on us generously through Jesus Christ our Savior" Titus 3:5.

The new birth comes through hearing and believing the gospel. "…faith comes from hearing the message, and the message is heard through the word of Christ" Romans 10:17.

The new birth comes by personally accepting Jesus. "Yet to all who received him, to those who believed in his name, he gave the right to become children of God" John 1:12. See also Acts 16:31.

What are the results of the new birth?
We become "children…born of God" John 1:13.

We are lived in by the Holy Spirit. "God's Spirit lives in you" 1 Corinthians 3:16.

We are "set free from the law of sin and death" Romans 8:2. "For what the law was powerless to do…God did by sending his own Son…to be a sin offering." Romans 8:3.

How can I be sure that I'm a Christian?

1 John

John is the only New Testament writer who tells us so explicitly why he wrote his Gospel and his first letter.

In the penultimate chapter of his Gospel he says that the miraculous signs which he did in the presence of his disciples, which are included in his Gospel, he has written "that you may believe that Jesus is the Christ, the Son of God, and that by believing you may have life in his name" John 20:31.

If the purpose of his Gospel was to help people believe in who Jesus was, the purpose of his first letter was to help people be certain about this. John states very clearly who his letter is addressed to. "I write these things to you who believe in the name of the Son of God." And what is John's reason for writing to these new Christians? "…so that you may know that you have eternal life" 1 John 5:13.

John uses the word "know" and words related to "know" over 40 times in his letter. "Everyone who loves has been born of God and knows God." 1 John 4:7.

A follow-up letter

John's first letter is the follow-up letter *par excellence*. It was written to Christians so that they could be sure that Jesus was God's Son and that their faith in him rested on solid rock. If anyone is ever asked to help brand new Christians then this is the letter to point them to.

Two things never to forget
1. The objective fact

We can be certain about our salvation because of what Jesus has done. It all depends, not on anything we may feel, or on anything that we might do, but on Jesus' completed work of atonement.

2. Our subjective experience

John also points out that we may be sure about our Christian faith because, along with all other Christian believers, the evidence of God's power will become increasingly evident in our lives, 1 John 2:3-5; 3:19-21.

1. Evidences of spiritual life

In studying 1 John there are five topics to be on the lookout for which have a direct bearing on Christian assurance.

The first concerns the long list of evidences of spiritual life in John's first letter. As each of these is identified, understood, and appropriated, so a new Christian becomes stronger and stronger in his or her faith.

- Life of a personal relationship with Jesus: 1:1, 2
- Life of fellowship: 1:3
    a. with fellow Christians
    b. with God the Father
    c. with God the Son
- Life of joy: 1:4
- Life of forgiveness: 1:9; 2:12
- Life of honesty: 1:8, 10
- Life of holiness 2:1
- Life of obedience 2:3; 5:2, 3

- Life of living in Jesus: 2:6
- Life of love: 2:10; 3:14; 4:7
- Life of victory over the evil one: 2:14; 5:4, 5
- Life of separation: 2:15, 17
- Life of perseverence: 2:19, 24
- Life of knowledge: 2:20; 5:20
- Life of anointing: 2:27
- Life of expectancy: 2:28
- Life of godliness: 2:29; 3:3
- Life of living in relationship with God: 3:1
- Life of anticipating Jesus' return: 3:2
- Life of hope: 3:3
- Life of doing what is right 3:10
- Life of sacrifice: 3:16
- Life of action: 3:18
- Life of good conscience: 3:21
- Life of confidence: 3:21
- Life of prayer: 3:22; 5:14, 15
- Life of recognizing God's Spirit: 4:2, 15
- Life of Jesus living in us: 4:4
- Life of truth: 4:6, 20
- Life of confidence: 4:17
- Life of lack of fear: 4:18
- Life of peace: 4:18
- Life of faith 5:4
- Life of assurance: 5:13
- Life of helping fellow-Christians: 5:16
- Life of safety: 5:18
- Life of reverence: 5:21

2. God's love for believers

In this letter John emphasizes the supreme characteristic of God: "God is love" 1 John 4:8.

a. The *direction* of God's love is towards us: 4:9
  b. The *dwelling* of God's love is in us: 4:16
  c. The *totality* of God's love is in us: 4:12

3. Can we expect sinless perfection?

One of the most subtle heresies in John's day, as in our day, is the notion that Christians will ever be sinless and perfect this side of heaven.

a. To say that I cannot sin is to deceive myself: 1:8
  b. To say that I have not sinned is to make God a liar: 1:10

4. The Holy Spirit in the life of a Christian

John teaches that no steps can be taken in the Christian life without the Holy Spirit, who initiates our walk with Jesus, continues to be with us each day, and will still live in us on the last day.

a. The Holy Spirit bears witness to Jesus' humanity and divinity: 4:2
  b. The Holy Spirit bears witness to the truth: 5:6, 8
  c. The Holy Spirit lives in a believer: 3:24
  d. The Holy Spirit confirms God's presence in us: 4:13
  e. The Holy Spirit anoints us: 2:20
  f. The Holy Spirit guides us into the truth: 4:6

5. Knowing God

John explains at great length about the one thing that should be uppermost in the mind of a new Christian: knowing God.

- We know God if we keep his commands: 2:3, 4
- We know God if we walk as Jesus did: 2:6
- We will be conscious that we live in the last hour: 2:18
- We will know the truth: 2:21
- Knowing God makes us do what is right: 2:29
- We know that when Jesus returns we will be like him: 3:2
- We know that Jesus came to take away our sins: 3:5
- We have the assurance that we have passed from death to life: 3:14
- We experience love for fellow-Christians: 3:14
- We know that we belong to the truth: 3:19
- We know that Jesus lives in us because of his Spirit: 3:24
- Because we know God we listen to him: 4:6
- We know that we love God's children by loving God: 5:2
- We know that we have eternal life: 5:13
- We know that our prayers will be answered: 5:14, 15
- We know that we will be victorious over Satan: 5:18
- We know that we are God's children: 5:19
- We know that Jesus has given us understanding: 5:20

Key words to study in 1 John
John gives basic teaching about seven themes in his first letter. Understanding each of them should increase our love for and knowledge of God.

1. Life
God's gift to the believer is life: 1:1, 2; 2:25; 3:14; 4:9; 5:11, 12.

2. Light and truth
Jesus came to give us light about God and his ways: 1:5-7; 2:8-11
  This means that we know the truth about many things: 1:8; 2:21, 27; 5:20.

3. Sin

John's teaching about sin if quite clear:
1:6, 8-10; 2:1; 3:4-6, 8; 5:16-18.

4. The world

Christians have to live in a godless
atmosphere: 2:2, 15-17; 3:13; 4:1, 3-5,
17; 5:4, 5, 19.

5. Abiding

Christians have a constant and
permanent relationship with Jesus: 2:6,
10, 24, 28: 3:6, 9, 15, 17, 24; 4:12, 13,
15, 16.

6. Born of God

Christians start the Christian life by a
spiritual birth: 2:29; 3:1, 2, 9, 19; 4:7;
5:2, 18. "Everyone who believes that
Jesus the Christ is born of God"
1 John 5:1.

7. Jesus Christ

John knows what false teachers are
saying about Jesus, so he sets out some
important teaching about who Jesus is:
1:1-3; 2:1, 22-24; 3:5, 7; 4:2, 3, 19, 14;
5:5, 6, 8; as well as about what Jesus has
done for us: 1:7; 2:2; 3:5, 8; 4:10.

2 GROWING IN THE CHRISTIAN LIFE

CONTENTS	
	page
INTRODUCTION	17
BIBLE READING	18-23
CHRISTIAN FELLOWSHIP	24-25
WORSHIP	26-27
KEY BIBLE VERSES FOR MY UNDERSTANDING ABOUT GOD	28
THE LOST ART OF MEDITATION ON GOD'S WORD	29
AVOIDING THE 30 THINGS THE BIBLE SAYS GOD HATES	30-31
SAYINGS OF JESUS TO APPLY TO YOUR HEART	32-35
32 KEY WAYS TO PLEASE GOD	36
APPLYING OLD TESTAMENT PROMISES TO DAILY LIVING	37-39
APPLYING PROMISES FROM THE PSALMS TO DAILY LIVING	40-41
MARTIN LUTHER AND PROMISES	42-43
APPLYING NEW TESTAMENT PROMISES TO DAILY LIVING	44-49
CHRISTIAN DISCIPLESHIP	50-51
HOW TO "ABIDE" IN JESUS	52-53

Introduction

It is often pointed out that Bible reading, prayer, Christian fellowship, worship and service are vital for anyone who wishes to grow as a Christian. In this section there are two Bible studies which enable you to give yourself a spiritual check-up. Then there are heart-warming Bible studies concentrating on God's promises.

Christians were born to grow. More of Paul's time was spent in encouraging Christians to become spiritually mature than on pioneer evangelism. Paul especially commended Epaphras for his earnest prayer that his fellow-Christians in Colosse should grow in maturity: "Epaphras, who is one of you and a servant of Christ Jesus, sends greetings. He is always wrestling in prayer for you, that you may stand firm in all the will of God, mature and fully assured" (Colossians 4:12). This is the purpose of the studies in this chapter.

Bible reading

Three stages
There are three stages in Bible reading:

1. the cod liver stage, when you take it like medicine;
2. the shredded wheat stage when it's nourishing but dry;
3. the peaches and cream stage when it is consumed with passion and pleasure.

The basics
Most Christians are aware of the basics about Bible reading:

- Pray before you start.
- See what the passages means in its own context.
- See what it teaches about:
  a. God (Father, Son and Holy Spirit)
  b. the Christian life.

Apply anything you have learned to your heart:

- Is there a command to obey?
- Is there a warning to heed?
- Is there a promise to claim?

End in prayer. However, daily Bible reading is harder to put into practice than is generally recognized. Two suggestions follow which are linked to this.

Preparing to read the Bible
The first way in which we may enhance our own reading of the Bible is to prepare ourselves for this. The Puritan divine, Thomas Watson, 1557–1592,

once listed 22 ways in which one should prepare for reading the Bible.

1. Remove hindrances

a. Remove the love of every sin.
b. Remove the distracting concerns of this world, especially covetousness: Matthew 13:22.
c. Don't make jokes with and out of Scripture.

2. Prepare your heart
See 1 Samuel 7:3. Do this by:

a. collecting your thoughts;
b. confessing to God any godless desires;
c. not coming to the Bible in a happy-go-lucky mood.

3. Read it with reverence
As you read believe that in each line God is speaking specifically to you.

4. Get a true understanding of Scripture

See Psalm 119:73. This is best achieved by comparing relevant parts of Scripture with each other.

5. Read the Bible in a serious frame of mind

See Deuteronomy 32:47. The Christian life is to be taken seriously since it requires effort, Luke 13:24, and care Hebrews 4:1.

6. Remember what you read

See Psalm 119:52. Don't allow it to be stolen from you, Matthew 13:4, 19. If what you read does not stay in your memory it is not likely to do you much good.

7. Meditate on what you read

See Psalm 119:15. The Hebrew word for "meditate" means "to be intense in the mind." Meditation without reading is wrong; reading without meditation is a barren and fruitless activity. Meditations should stir the affections so that you will be warmed by its heat. See Psalm 39:3.

8. Read with a humble heart

Acknowledge that you are not worthy that God should reveal himself to you, James 4:6.

9. Believe that all of the Bible is God's holy Word

See 2 Timothy 3:16. We know that no sinner could have written it because of the way it describes sin. No saint could commit such a blasphemy against God by substituting his own words for God's Word.

10. Prize the Bible highly

See Psalm 119:72. It is your lifeline; you were born through it, James 1:18. You need to grow by reading it, 1 Peter 2:2.

11. Love the Bible with all your heart

See Psalm 119:159.

12. Read the Bible with an honest heart

See Luke 8:15.

  a. Be prepared to know the whole of God's will.
  b. Be prepared to be changed by what you read in the Bible, John 17:17.

13. Apply to yourself everything that you read

View every word as if it was spoken to you. Take its condemnation of sins as the condemnation of your own sin.

14. Note its commands as much as its promises

Remember that you need direction just as much as you need comfort.

15. Don't be absorbed in too many minor details

But pay close attention to the important things, Hosea 8:12.

16. Compare yourself with the Word

How do you compare?

17. Pay special attention to those passages that speak to your individual, particular and present circumstances

  a. Affliction: see Hebrews 12:7; Isaiah 27:9; John 16:20; 2 Corinthians 4:17.
  b. A sense of Christ's presence being withdrawn: see Isaiah 54:8; 57:16; Psalm 97:11.
  c. Sin: see Galatians 5:24; James 1:15; 1 Peter 2:11; Proverbs 7:10, 22, 23; Proverbs 22:14.
  d. Unbelief: see Isaiah 26:3; 2 Samuel 22:31; John 3:15, 1 John 5:10; 3:36.

18. Pay special attention to the examples of people in the Bible as if they were living sermons

  a. Punishments: see Nebuchadnezzar, Herod: Numbers 25:3, 4, 9; 1 Kings 14:9, 10; Acts 5:5, 10; 1 Corinthians 10:11; Jude 7.
  b. Deliverances: See Daniel and Jeremiah, and the three young men in the furnace.

19. Don't stop reading the Bible until you find your heart warmed
See Psalm 119:93. Let the Bible not only inform you but let it set you on fire, Jeremiah 23:29; Luke 24:32.

20. Put into practice what you read
See Psalm 119:66, 105; Deuteronomy 17:19.

21. For us Jesus is Prophet, Priest and King
Make use of his office as a Prophet,

Revelation 5:5; John 8:12; Psalm 119:102, 103. Ask Jesus not only to open up the Scriptures to you, but to open up your mind and understanding, Luke 24:45.

22. Pray that you will benefit from your reading
See Isaiah 48:17; Psalm 119:18; Nehemiah 9:20.

The Bible is...
If we recall what the Bible is we should find that we read it more regularly. Here are 18 facts about God's Word:

  1. Humans do not live just by bread but by every word that comes from God: Deuteronomy 8:3.
  2. God's Word is so close to you, in your mouth and in your heart, that you must obey it: Deuteronomy 30:14.
  3. God's Word is right and true: Psalm 33:4.
  4. God's Word created the universe: Psalm 33:6; Hebrews 11:3.
  5. Angels obey God's Word: Psalm 103:20.
  6. God healed his people by his Word: Psalm 107:20.
  7. God's Word is permanent: Psalm 119:89.
  8. God's Word is true: Psalm 119:160.
  9. God's Word and name are exalted above everything else: Psalm 138:2.
  10. God's Word comes to us quickly: Psalm 147:15.

11. Every word of God is pure: Proverbs 30:5.
12. God's Word is like fire: Jeremiah 23:29.
13. Everything that God's Word prophecies will be fulfilled: Ezekiel 12:25.
14. God's Word, Jesus, became a human being and lived a human life: John 1:14.
15. God's Word is the sword of the Spirit: Ephesians 6:17.
16. God's Word is not chained: 2 Timothy 2:9.
17. Hebrews 4:12 says that God's Word:
    a. is living
    b. is active
    c. is sharper than any double-edged sword
    d. can penetrate the soul and spirit, joints and marrow
    e. judges the thoughts and attitudes of the heart.
18. God's Word endures: 1 Peter 1:23.

What does reading the Bible do?

The Bible helps the Christian in countless different ways. Here are some of the ways in which the Bible can help a Christian to grow spiritually.

1. The Bible testifies to Jesus: John 5:39.
2. The Bible searches the heart: Hebrews 4:12.
3. The Bible can keep a young person's life pure: Psalm 119:9.
4. The Bible is like a light guiding us: Psalm 119:105.
5. The Bible will bring about what it promises: Isaiah 55:11.
6. The Bible makes us wise about salvation: 2 Timothy 3:15.
7. Reading the Bible produces belief that Jesus is the Christ: John 20:31.
8. The Bible makes the simple wise: Psalm 19:7.
9. The Bible makes Christians grow: 1 Peter 2:2; Hebrews 5:12-14.
10. The Bible builds us up: Acts 20:32.
11. The Bible teaches us by its warnings: 1 Corinthians 10:11.
12. The Bible instills obedience in us: Deuteronomy 17:19, 20.
13. The Bible makes us holy: John 17:17; Ephesians 5:26.
14. The Bible makes us effective in his service: 1 Thessalonians 2:13; Colossians 3:16.
15. The Bible produces hope: Psalm 119:49; Romans 15:4.
16. The Bible brings comfort: Psalm 119:82.

17. The Bible makes the heart rejoice:
    Psalm 19:8; 119:111.
18. The Bible teaches us about Christian
    doctrine: 2 Timothy 3:16.
19. The Bible helps us in personal
    evangelism: Luke 8:11-15.
20. The Bible helps us to live fruitful
    lives: John 15:3, 5, 7.
21. The Bibles gives us victory over
    Satan: Matthew 4:4;
    Ephesians 6:11, 17.
22. The Bible gives us assurance about
    heaven: John 14:1-3.

Spiritual nourishment

The Bible is full of spiritual food. It is
likened to:

1. milk, 1 Peter 2:2
2. bread, Matthew 4:4
3. meat, Hebrews 5:12-14
4. honey, Psalm 19:10; 119:103.

The author of the letter to the Hebrews
rebukes his readers for imbibing milk
when they should have been weaned
long ago and have moved on to eating
meaty steaks.

Bible reading and the family

It is clear that Timothy was blessed by
being born into a godly family. His
mother and grandmother both loved
God. "I have been reminded of your
sincere faith, which first lived in your
grandmother, Lois and in your mother
Eunice and, I am persuaded, now lives
in you also" 2 Timothy 1:5.

Paul notes that Timothy, like all other

Jewish children, was taught from the
scriptures from an early age. "…and how
from infancy you have known the holy
Scriptures, which are able to make you
wise for salvation through faith in Christ
Jesus" 2 Timothy 3:15.

From about 164 BC, the Pharisee
Simeon ben Shetah ordered that all
Jewish boys should attend the "house of
the book" where they would receive a
Jewish education. From about the age of
six Jesus would have gone to the "house
of the book" in Nazareth. There a
teacher, paid for by the synagogue,
would have used what we now know as
the Old Testament, as his text book.

Much of the learning was done by
repetition. This method of teaching by
rote is referred to in Isaiah 28:9-10,
where the people are complaining that
Isaiah is treating them like children:
"Who is it he is trying to teach? To
whom is he explaining his message. To
children weaned from their milk, to
those just taken from the breast? For it
is: Do and do, do and do, rule on rule,
rule on rule, a little here, a little there."
This literally means, "s after s, q after q,"
referring to teaching by repetition. The
teacher would say the letter s and the
school children would repeat the letter s
after him. Jewish boys were taught the
Scriptures in a systematic way.

Today, where few schools exist which
teach the Bible so faithfully, it is the
responsibility of every church fellowship
to encourage the reading of the Bible in
the home.

Christian fellowship

Koinonia

The Greek word for fellowship, *koinonia*, is translated by a number of words: "sharing," "partnership," and "contribution," as well as by the word "fellowship."

Called into fellowship

Paul states that, "God, who has called you into fellowship with his Son Jesus Christ our Lord, is faithful" 1 Corinthians 1:9. The foundation for all genuine Christian fellowship is based on the individual's faith in Jesus.

Fellowship and forgiveness

The apostle John emphasizes another facet of fellowship in 1 John 1:7: "If we walk in the light, as he [God] is in the light, we have fellowship with one another, and the blood of Jesus, his Son, purifies us from all sin." Before we can have true fellowship with fellow-

Christians we must have confessed any known sin to God, so that we can truly say that we are walking in the light.

Acts 2:42

The best description of Christian fellowship in the New Testament describes the fellowship which the early church experienced.

"They devoted themselves to:
the apostles' teaching
and to the fellowship,
to the breaking of bread
and to prayer."

Thanks to their wholehearted practice of Christian fellowship the early Christians were knit into a close-knit and loving community. "They broke bread in their homes and ate together with glad and sincere hearts, praising God and enjoying the favor of all the people. And the Lord added to their number daily..." Acts 2:46-47.

Enhancing our fellowship with God
Fellowship with God has been called
"walking with God." Enoch is perhaps
the most striking example of this.
"Enoch walked with God; then he was
no more, because God took him away"
Genesis 5:24.

1. The need for discipline in the fellowship
When Paul wrote to the Corinthian
church, which was brimming over with
charismatic gifts, he nevertheless did not
shrink from telling them that they were
wrong not to expel from their fellowship
people who were openly indulging in a
kind of sexual immorality that even the
pagans did not indulge in,
1 Corinthians 5:1-2.

2. The need for a Spirit-filled fellowship
The one outstanding characteristic of
Christian fellowship, which should
distinguish it from all other kinds of
groups, is that it is full of God's Spirit.
See 2 Corinthians 13:14; Philippians 2:1.

3. The need for a warm-hearted fellowship
Humanly speaking if it had not been for
Barnabas Paul would not have been
welcomed into the Christian fellowship.
When Paul went to Jerusalem he
attempted to join the fellowship of the
disciples. But they cold-shouldered him
as they were afraid of him. They knew
that he had been fanatical in his

persecution of the Christians. They
certainly were not prepared to give him
the benefit of the doubt. They could not
bring themselves to believe that he was a
genuine disciple of Jesus, see Acts 9:26.
But Barnabas came to the rescue. He
himself took Paul to the apostles. He
told them about Paul's Damascus Road
conversion, and how he was now
preaching fearlessly in the name of Jesus,
see Acts 9:27. As a result of Barnabas'
action Paul was then accepted into the
Christian fellowship.

This made a great impact on Paul and
he never forgot the role of Barnabas in
this. Paul referred to this incident in
Galatians 2:9, "James, Peter, and John,
those reputed to be pillars, gave me and
Barnabas the right hand of fellowship
when they recognized the grace given
to me."

Today, for one reason or another most
Christian fellowships have members who
feel that they are not valued. Each
fellowship needs its Barnabas.

4. The need for a sympathetic fellowship
Paul was not slow to praise the good
points in the fellowship of Christians at
Corinth. Paul was so grateful to them that
they shared in all his suffering, see
2 Corinthians 1:7. Paul knew that they
were one with him in all his hardships
and persecution. This kind of fellowship
from new, young Christians, was greatly
appreciated by the seasoned, battle-
scarred apostle. See 2 Corinthians 1:8-11.

Worship

No optional extra

Some Christians think that public worship is not essential. Some would even go so far as to say that it is an optional extra.

For Jesus, public worship involved going to far from perfect synagogues. "He [Jesus] went to Nazareth, where he had been brought up, and on the Sabbath day he went into the synagogue, *as was his custom*" Luke 4:16.

For Peter and John, public worship meant going to the temple, "at the time of prayer–at three in the afternoon" Acts 3:1. The early Christians enjoyed close fellowship among themselves, but did not neglect attending public worship.

Taking public worship seriously

"Whenever we fail to take public worship seriously, we are less than the fully biblical Christians we claim to be. We go to church for the preaching, some of us say, not for the praise. Evangelism is our speciality, not worship. In consequence either our worship services are slovenly, perfunctory, mechanical and dull or, in an attempt to remedy this, we go to the opposite extreme and become repetitive, unreflective and even flippant." *John Stott*

It is little wonder that Martin Luther once said that "to believe God is to worship God."

Why is public worship so important?

There are frequent warnings, especially by the New Testament prophets, about

the danger of insincere worship and the worship of idols, see Exodus 20:4; Deuteronomy 4:28; Isaiah 40:20; 1 Corinthians 8:4.

However, in addition to the example of Jesus and the apostles, there are a number of good reasons for attending public worship regularly.

1. God commanded it

The pattern of worship centered on the tabernacle is meant to be a model about the necessity for worshiping God. "But you are to seek the place the Lord your God will choose from among all your

tribes to put his Name there for his dwelling. To that place you must go" Deuteronomy 12:5.

Also in Deuteronomy 16:16 all Jewish men were specifically told to be present at three feasts: The Feast of Unleavened Bread, the Feast of Weeks, and the Feast of Tabernacles.

2. Worship brings blessing

This is hardly the prime motivation for going to church. However, it is a wonderful fact that as we worship God we are spiritually blessed. "Blessed are those who dwell in your house; they are

ever praising you" Psalm 122:4.

3. Worship in a crisis

When we go through a time of trouble, that is not the time to withdraw from public worship. Rather it is a time to draw strength from being with others as they sing God's praises. On hearing the news that Jerusalem was likely to be defeated, King Hezekiah tore his clothes and put on sackcloth, two symbols of mourning and repentance, and then "went to the temple of the Lord" Isaiah 37:1.

4. Worship and teaching

Arguments rage over whether worship should include a time of instruction or whether the time of instruction should be separate from worship. Whatever is decided there is no getting away from the importance of a time of instruction being part of a Christian's staple diet. "Come, let us go to the mountain of the Lord, to the house of the God of Jacob. He will teach us his ways, so that we may walk in his paths" Micah 4:2.

5. Worship will be the way of life in heaven

The book of Revelation reveals that the main activity in heaven will be worshiping God. See Revelation 4:8, 11; 5:9-14; 7:9-17; 11:16-18; 12:10-12; 15:3, 4; 16:5-7; 19:1-8.

"Hallelujah! Salvation and glory and power belong to our God" Revelation 19:1.

Key Bible verses for my understanding about God

Proverbs

The book of Proverbs is not the only place in the Bible to look for helpful proverbs. The New Testament is full of proverbs. One of the best ways to grow in our Christian lives is to forget ourselves and focus our attention on God and his greatness. The following 20 New Testament "proverbs" remind us about our wonderful God.

1. God's blessings fall on everyone: Matthew 5:45.
2. God, the creator of the universe, brings light into the world with Jesus: John 1:1-5.
3. God orders everyone to repent: Acts 26:8.
4. God does raise the dead, so why is that thought to be incredible?: Acts 26:8.
5. God is clearly seen in creation: Romans 1:20.
6. God's so-called foolishness is wiser than any human wisdom: 1 Corinthians 1:25.
7. God's so-called weakness is stronger than human strength: 1 Corinthians 1:25.
8. God has given us the guarantee of his Spirit in our hearts: 2 Corinthians 1:22.
9. All the treasures of wisdom and knowledge are found in God: Colossians 2:2-3.
10. God has given us the gift of salvation in Jesus: 1 Thessalonians 5:9.
11. God is just: 2 Thessalonians 1:6.
12. In the life of Jesus God became visible: 1 Timothy 3:16.
13. God resists the proud but welcomes the humble: 1 Peter 5:5.
14. To God, one day is like a thousand years: 2 Peter 3:8.
15. God never forgets his promises: 2 Peter 3:9.
16. God is light: 1 John 1:5.
17. Out of his great love, God calls us his children: 1 John 3:1.
18. Once we are God's we are more powerful than all the forces in the world: 1 John 4:4.
19. Even before we ever loved God, he loved us and sent Jesus to us: 1 John 4:10.
20. Because God loved us first we now love him: 1 John 4:19.

The lost art of meditation on God's Word

The psalmist

This has been called "the lost art" among Christians. But for the psalmist it was an integral part of his spiritual life. He meditated on:

- God's unfailing love: Psalm 48:9
- God's precepts: Psalm 119:15
- all of God's works: Psalm 77:12
- God's promises: Psalm 119:148.

For the psalmist, meditation was not something that he only did occasionally or at special times. The psalmist meditated day and night, Psalm 1:2.

Four kinds of contemplation

Bernard of Clairvaux, 1090–1153, the Abbot of Clairvaux, and author of a monastic Rule and several devotional books, encouraged his monks to meditate in the following four ways.

1. Meditate on God's majesty

"The first and the greatest way to contemplate is to wonder at God's majesty. This demands a heart made pure, so that freed from vices and released from sin, it can ascend easily to heavenly things. Sometimes this contemplation holds the watcher rapt in amazement and ecstasy, if only for a moment."

2. Meditate on God's judgments

"A second kind of contemplation is necessary for this man. He needs to look on the judgments of God. While this contemplation strikes fear into the onlooker because it is indeed frightening, it drives out vices, strengthens virtues, initiates wisdom, protects humility. Humility is the true and solid foundation of virtues. For if humility were to collapse, the building-up of the virtues will fall down."

3. Meditate on God's kindness with gratitude

"The third kind of contemplation is occupied (or rather at leisure) in remembering kindnesses and, so that it avoids ingratitude. It urges him who remembers to love his Benefactor. Of such says the prophet, speaking to the Lord, 'They will celebrate your abundant goodness and joyfully sing of your righteousness' Psalm 145:7."

4. Meditate on God's promises

"The fourth contemplation, which forgets what is past, rests wholly in the expectation of what is promised, Philippians 3:13, which nourishes patience and nerves the arm of perseverance, for what is promised is eternal." *Bernard of Clairvaux*

Avoiding the 30 things the Bible says God hates

Negative and positive

There is a negative side and a positive side to holiness. There are prohibitions to be heeded as well as commands to be followed in the Christian life. Unpopular as they may be, here are 30 things to be avoided if we want to grow in the Christian life.

Some of the things on the list below may seem to be a bit far-fetched or have nothing to do with us in the twenty-first century. However, this is far from the truth. For example, it was reported in February, 2002, that two young people who were on trial in Germany had engaged in a human sacrifice.

30 things God hates

1. God hates idol worship: Deuteronomy 7:25.
2. God hates the worship of the sun, moon or stars: Deuteronomy 17:3.
3. God hates human sacrifice: Deuteronomy 18:10.
4. God hates divination: Deuteronomy 18:10.
5. God hates sorcery: Deuteronomy 18:10.
6. God hates omens: Deuteronomy 18:10.
7. God hates witchcraft: Deuteronomy 18:10.
8. God hates people who cast spells: Deuteronomy 18:11.
9. God hates mediums: Deuteronomy 18:11.
10. God hates spiritists: Deuteronomy 18:11.
11. God hates those who consult the dead: Deuteronomy 18:11.
12. God hates dishonest business practice: Deuteronomy 25:13-16.
13. God hates all wrong-doing: Psalm 5:5.
14. God hates the wicked: Psalm 11:5.
15. God hates those who love violence: Psalm 11:5.
16. God hates people who are perverse: Proverbs 3:32.
17. God hates a proud look: Proverbs 6:16.
18. God hates a lying tongue: Proverbs 6:17.
19. God hates those who kill innocent people: Proverbs 6:17.
20. God hates those who devise wicked schemes: Proverbs 6:18.
21. God hates people who rush to do evil: Proverbs 6:18.
22. God hates a false witness: Proverbs 6:18.
23. God hates a person who stirs up dissension in his family: Proverbs 6:18.
24. God hates the thoughts of the wicked: Proverbs 15:26.
25. God hates the proud of heart: Proverbs 16:5.
26. God hates those who acquit the guilty but condemn the innocent: Proverbs 17:15.
27. God hates insincere worship: Isaiah 1:13.
28. God hates robbery: Isaiah 61:8.
29. God hates those who plot evil against their neighbors: Zechariah 8:17.
30. God hates divorce: Malachi 2:14-16.

The pharisaical approach

There is little point in running down the above list and putting a tick against each one that we have not indulged in today, if we then think to ourselves: What a good person am I! For one of the greatest sins that is constantly referred to in the Bible is pride. And no one feels able to say that they are never proud.

The point about the above list is that there are some things in the Christian life which are right and some things which are wrong. Nobody who wants to grow into spiritual maturity will want to hang on to things which are definitely out for a Christian.

Sins mentioned in the Bible

It is easy to read the Bible as if it does not always apply to us. Most of the warnings about particular sins are given

as warnings to believers. To be rid of sins in our own lives we first of all have to identify them and own up to them. Many of the sins mentioned in the Bible are ones we find easy to see in others but which we are much slower to see in ourselves.

Here are 13 ways in which sin often shows itself:

1. disobeying God's commandments: Exodus 20:3-17; James 2:10
2. self-righteousness: Galatians 6:3; Isaiah 5:21
3. the wrong sort of ambition: Mark 9:33-35
4. pride: Psalm 12:4
5. criticizing others: Luke 6:41
6. bitterness: Ephesians 4:31
7. rage and anger: Ephesians 4:31
8. brawling and slander: Ephesians 4:31
9. malice: Ephesians 4:31
10. envy: James 3:14
11. biting and devouring fellow-Christians: Galatians 5:15
12. flattery: Proverbs 29:5
13. hypocrisy: Titus 1:16

When we are prepared to admit to ourselves what terribly unchristian thoughts we have, and how dreadful some of our actions have been, we have taken the first step in our battle against sin.

We are in good company in this struggle. Even the great apostle Paul wrote: "For what I do is not the good I want to do; no, the evil I do not want to do–this I keep doing" Romans 7:19.

Sayings of Jesus to apply to your heart

Role model

Jesus is the role model for the Christian. He never wrote a book but the four Gospels have recorded all of his teaching which we need to know if we are seeking to make progress in our walk with God. If there is one part of Scripture that Christians should meditate on it is the words of Jesus.

Jesus' sayings in Matthew's Gospel

1. Jesus can help us in personal evangelism: Matthew 4:19.
2. Jesus promised to bless peacemakers: Matthew 5:11.
3. We are meant to shine like lights: Matthew 5:16.
4. We are told to put right any arguments before we worship: Matthew 5:24, 25.
5. We are meant to be generous with our possessions: Matthew 5:40.
6. We have to go the second mile: Matthew 5:42.
7. We have to love people who may never return our love: Matthew 5:46, 47.
8. When we give money to God's work it should be done discreetly: Matthew 6:2.
9. We should not parade ourselves when we pray: Matthew 6:5.
10. Before we ask for God's forgiveness of us we must forgive others: Matthew 6:14.
11. When we fast we must not draw attention to this fact: Matthew 6:16.
12. We must not sit in judgment on others: Matthew 7:1.
13. We must not point out other people's faults before we have corrected our own: Matthew 7:5.
14. We must not throw pearls to pigs: Matthew 7:6.
15. We must do to other people as we wish them to do to us: Matthew 7:12.
16. We can identify false prophets by their fruits: Matthew 7:20.
17. As we have received God's free grace, so we must give freely: Matthew 10:8.
18. We should be wise as serpents and as harmless as doves: Matthew 10:16.
19. If we are persecuted we need not worry about what we should say to our persecutors, for God will provide us with the necessary words: Matthew 10:17-19.
20. We should not be surprised if non-Christians hate us, but we should persevere in our Christian walk to the end of our lives: Matthew 10:22.
21. When we are persecuted we should be more concerned about the eternal welfare of our souls than about anything that people do to our bodies: Matthew 10:28.
22. We should witness to people about God, knowing that we will then be acknowledged by God in heaven: Matthew 10:32.
23. We should make God the number

one priority in our lives, even above our family: Matthew 10:37.

24. We should be especially kind to people who are unrecognized by the world: Matthew 10:42.

25. We should help the marginalized as if we were helping Jesus himself: Matthew 18:5.

26. We must never put a stumbling-block in the way of those who are God's "little ones." It would be better to be executed than to do this: Matthew 18:6.

27. If a fellow-Christian harms us we should have it out with him first of all, and try and win him over. If that fails we can challenge him before a couple of believers. Only if that fails as well should we tell the whole fellowship. If he does not listen to them he should be treated as an outcast: Matthew 18:15-17.

28. Even when we are praying with just one or two other Christians we should remember that God listens to us: Matthew 18:19.

29. We should not put a limit on the number of times we are prepared to forgive a Christian who wrongs us: Matthew 18:21, 22.

30. Whether we remain single or marry we should do so for the sake of the kingdom of God. We must remember that celibacy is a gift from God which is not given to everyone: Matthew 19:11, 12.

31. We should never get in the way of

children coming to Jesus: Matthew 19:14, 15.

32. Whatever we give up for God in this life will be more than amply rewarded in the next life: Matthew 19:29.

33. We should follow the example of Jesus and be a servant to everyone: Matthew 20:27, 28.

34. We should give to the state what is due to the state, and give to God what is due to God: Matthew 22:21.

35. We must remember that heaven will exceed all human relationships, even marriage: Matthew 22:30.

36. We must love our neighbors as we love ourselves: Matthew 22:39.

37. We must not push ourselves forward but be humble. Then God will exalt us: Matthew 23:12.

38. We should never act in a violent way in an effort to promote God's kingdom: Matthew 26:52.

39. We should engage in evangelism in God's name: Matthew 28:19, 20.

Jesus' sayings in Mark's Gospel

1. We are to tell our family about what Jesus has done for us and about his compassion: Mark 5:19.
2. We are not to be surprised if we find that our family do not listen to us when we talk about Jesus: Mark 6:4.
3. We should not object to evangelism by Christians who belong to a different group from us: Mark 9:38, 39.
4. We must recall that Jesus asks some people to give up their wealth and give it away to the poor, as part of their Christian discipleship: Mark 10:21.
5. We must not parade our spirituality: Mark 12:38-40.

Jesus' sayings in Luke's Gospel

1. In Jesus' presence we must remember how sinful we are, and yet how he commissioned Peter to engage in personal evangelism: Luke 5:8-10.
2. We must recall that it is not wrong to do good on a Sunday: Luke 6:9.
3. We must remember that it is a bad sign if everyone says how marvelous we are: Luke 6:26.
4. We must love our enemies, even if they harm us: Luke 6:27, 28.
5. We must be generous to those who will never pay us back: Luke 6:34, 35.
6. We must be merciful towards others, just as God the Father is merciful towards us: Luke 6:36.
7. Our lives should be characterized by generosity. We will be rewarded and receive more than we have ever given: Luke 6:38.
8. We should be like the Good Samaritan: Luke 10:36, 37.
9. We should be alert to being covetous: Luke 12:15.
10. We should be humble and not try and take pride of place on any occasion: Luke 14:8-10.
11. We should be hospitable, not just to our own family and friends, but to the poor and disadvantaged: Luke 14:13, 14.
12. We should not grumble about anyone coming to Jesus later on in life: Luke 15:31, 32.

Jesus' sayings in John's Gospel

1. We should emulate Jesus washing the disciples' feet and be glad to engage in humble service: John 13:14.
2. We should do whatever Jesus tells us to do: John 15:14.
3. We should give spiritual food to God's people: John 21:15.

The teaching of Jesus

"The teaching of Christ is more excellent that all the advice of the saints, and he who has his spirit will find in it a hidden manna."
Thomas à Kempis

32 key ways to please God

Pleasing God

There are a host of specific things which God calls on Christians to do if they want to please him.

1. Seek first God's kingdom and his righteousness: Matthew 6:33.
2. Pray for more workers to work in God's harvest field: Matthew 9:38.
3. Worship God in the right way, in spirit and in truth: John 4:24.
4. Obey God rather than men: Acts 5:29.
5. Present your bodies to God as a living sacrifice: Romans 12:1.
6. Honor God with your body: 1 Corinthians 6:20.
7. Be eager for spiritual gifts: 1 Corinthians 14:1.
8. Stand firm in the Christian faith: 1 Corinthians 16:13.
9. Do not grieve the Holy Spirit: Ephesians 4:30.
10. Be filled with the Holy Spirit: Ephesians 5:18.
11. Rejoice in the Lord: Philippians 3:1.
12. Set your hearts on things above, not on earthly things: Colossians 3:1, 2.
13. Let Jesus' peace rule in your hearts: Colossians 3:15.
14. Let Jesus' word live in you: Colossians 3:16.
15. Do everything in the name of Jesus: Colossians 3:17.
16. Don't stop praying: 1 Thessalonians 5:17.
17. Give thanks to God about everything: 1 Thessalonians 5:18.
18. Don't neglect the gift God has given you: 1 Timothy 4:14.
19. Don't be ashamed about witnessing about Jesus: 2 Timothy 1:8.
20. Work hard to enter in the rest God has prepared for his followers: Hebrews 4:11.
21. Hang on to the hope you have: Hebrews 10:23.
22. Live your life by faith: Hebrews 10:38.
23. Don't resent God's discipline: Hebrews 12:5.
24. Humbly receive God's word: James 1:21.
25. Submit yourself to God: James 4:7.
26. If you are in trouble, pray: James 5:13.
27. If you are happy, sing God's praises: James 5:13.
28. Cast your anxiety on God: 1 Peter 5:7.
29. Build yourself up in your holy faith: Jude 20.
30. When you fall, repent: Revelation 2:5.
31. Fear God and give him glory: Revelation 14:7.
32. Worship God the Creator: Revelation 14:7.

Applying Old Testament promises to daily living

Apply

For many people the words of the Old Testament are no more than dry as dust history. But when God's Spirit takes them and applies them to our hearts and our present situation they come alive.

The way to derive the most benefit from the list below is to look up the verse in your Bible and note the context in which it comes. The first verse was spoken by David when he was thanking God for a recent deliverance from his enemies. Having found that out you could use the theme of the verse to thank God for the way he has delivered you from something specific in your life. In this way each verse can be applied to something that has happened, or is happening, or you expect to happen in your own life.

Promises from God and statements about God

1. God's way is perfect: 2 Samuel 22:31.
2. God judges the world in righteousness: Psalm 9:8.
3. In times of trouble, God will be your refuge: Psalm 9:9.
4. The Lord is King for ever and ever: Psalm 10:18.
5. The Lord loves righteousness: Psalm: 11:7.
6. The heavens show the glory of God: Psalm 19:1.
7. God gives his people the blessing of peace: Psalm 29:11.
8. God brings wars to an end: Psalm 46:9.
9. God is for you: Psalm 56:9.
10. God will not break his covenant: Psalm 89:34.
11. The Lord knows your thoughts: Psalm 94:11.
12. God's faithfulness continues through all generations: Psalm 100:5.
13. The Lord is compassionate: Psalm 103:8.
14. The Lord is gracious: Psalm 103:8.
15. The Lord is slow to anger: Psalm 103:8.
16. The Lord abounds in love: Psalm 103:8.
17. In the Lord's sight the death of his saints is precious: Psalm 116:15.
18. The Lord's love fills the world: Psalm 119:64.
19. When God's word enters your life it gives you understanding: Psalm 119:130.
20. God does not sleep but watches over his people: Psalm 121:4.
21. Children are God's gift: Psalm 127:3.
22. The Lord is good: Psalm 135:3.
23. It is impossible to escape from God's presence: Psalm 139:7, 8.
24. Love covers all sins: Proverbs 10:12.
25. God's word stands for ever: Isaiah 40:8.
26. God's salvation lasts for ever: Isaiah 51:6.
27. God's righteousness will never fail: Isaiah 51:6.
28. The Lord's word will achieve what it was sent for: Isaiah 55:11.
29. The Lord is mighty: Zepheniah 3:17.
30. The Lord never changes: Malachi 3:6.

TAKING HOLD OF GOD'S PROMISES		
The promise	*The condition*	*The reference*
1. It will go well with you.	Keeping God's commands.	Deuteronomy 6:3
2. God will honor…	…those who honor him.	1 Samuel 2:30
3. The Lord is with you…	…when you are with him.	1 Chronicles 15:2
4. The Lord will be found.	If you seek him.	1 Chronicles 15:2
5. God will guide you.	If you don't trust your own understanding	Proverbs 3:5, 6
6. You will become wise.	By walking with the wise	Proverbs 13:20
7. You will be blessed.	If you are kind to the poor.	Proverbs 14:21
8. You will turn away anger.	By a gentle answer.	Proverbs 15:1
9. Your plans will succeed.	If you commit everything to God.	Proverbs 16:3
10. You will avoid evil.	If you fear the Lord.	Proverbs 16:6
11. You will find life, prosperity and honor.	If you follow righteousness and love.	Proverbs 21:21
12. You will avoid calamity.	If you guard your tongue.	Proverbs 21:23
13. You will have wealth, honor and life.	If you are humble and fear the Lord.	Proverbs 22:4
14. You will recover after many falls.	If you are righteous.	Proverbs 24:16
15. You will be kept safe.	If you trust in the Lord.	Proverbs 29:25
16. God will give you wisdom.	If you please him.	Ecclesiastes 2:26
17. You will be kept in perfect peace.	If you trust in the Lord.	Isaiah 26:3
18. God will bless you.	If you wait for him	Isaiah 30:18
19. Your strength will be renewed.	If you hope in the Lord.	Isaiah 40:13
20. You will receive the Lord's mercy.	If you turn to the Lord.	Isaiah 55:7
21. Your spirit will be revived.	If you are humble.	Isaiah 57:15
22. You will find rest for your soul	If you walk in the good way.	Jeremiah 6:16
23. God will be with you.	If you obey him.	Jeremiah 7:23
24. God will tell you great things.	If you call on him.	Jeremiah 33:3
25. God will return to you.	If you return to him.	Malachi 3:16
26. You will leap like calves.	If you revere God's name.	Malachi 4:2

Taking hold of God's promises

Many of God's promises have conditions attached to them. We need to remember that it is essential that we fulfil these conditions. This is the way in which we take hold of God's wonderful promises. The promises on page 38, all taken from the Old Testament, have conditions attached to them.

Old Testament warnings to heed

The Bible is full of warnings as well as promises. The warnings from the Old Testament that follow also have conditions attached to them. The first one, for example, explains in what circumstances the Lord will forsake us. He does this if we forsake him. "If you forsake him, he will forsake you."

	OLD TESTAMENT WARNINGS TO HEED		
	The warning	*The condition*	*The reference*
1.	The Lord will forsake you.	If you forsake the Lord.	2 Chronicles 15:2
2.	The Lord will not listen to you.	If you cherish sin in your heart.	Psalm 66:18
3.	You will build your house in vain.	Unless the Lord builds it.	Psalm 127:1
4.	You will be immersed in quarrels.	If you are proud.	Proverbs 13:10
5.	Evil will never leave your house.	If you repay good with evil.	Proverbs 17:13
6.	You will not prosper.	If you conceal your sins.	Proverbs 18:13
7.	You will fall into trouble.	If you harden your heart.	Proverbs 28:14
8.	You will cast off restraint.	If you do not keep God's law.	Proverbs 29:18

Applying promises from the Psalms to daily living

The Psalms

The Psalms have more teaching about God than any other book of the Bible. Statements about God as well as specific promises to God's followers, most often with conditions attached, appear on almost every page.

A psalm

"What is more pleasing than a psalm? A psalm is a blessing on the lips of the people, praise of God, the assembly's homage, a general acclamation, a word that speaks for all, the voice of the Church, a confession of faith in song." *Ambrose*

THE PSALMS		
The promise	*The condition*	*The reference*
1. You will be like a fruitful tree.	If you delight in God's law.	Psalm 1:1-3
2. The Lord will hear you.	When you call to him.	Psalm 4:3
3. You will live in the Lord's sanctuary.	If you lead a blameless life.	Psalm 15:1, 2
4. God will keep you safe.	When you take refuge in him.	Psalm 16:1
5. You will not be shaken.	If you set the Lord always before you.	Psalm 16:8
6. You will be filled with God's joy.	If you are in his presence.	Psalm 16:11
7. The Lord will reward you...	...according to your righteousness.	Psalm 18:20
8. God shows that he is faithful...	...to those who are faithful to him.	Psalm 18:25
9. You will be greatly rewarded...	...if you keep God's commands.	Psalm 19:11
10. You will not be in want...	...if the Lord is your shepherd.	Psalm 23:1
11. You may stand in God's holy place...	...if you are pure.	Psalm 24:4
12. God will guide...	...if you are humble.	Psalm 25:9
13. God will instruct you...	...if you fear him.	Psalm 25:12
14. You will be strong...	...if you wait for the Lord.	Psalm 27:14
15. You will be blessed by God.	When you have no deceit.	Psalm 32:2
16. The Lord's love will surround you.	When you trust him.	Psalm 32:10
17. God will be your help and shield.	When you hope in him.	Psalm 33:20
18. You will be delivered from your fears.	When you seek the Lord.	Psalm 34:4
19. God's angel will deliver you.	When you fear the Lord.	Psalm 34:7

20. You will experience the Lord's goodness.	When you take refuge in him.	Psalm 34:8
21. You will lack nothing.	If you fear the Lord.	Psalm 34:9
22. You will be delivered from all your troubles.	If you are righteous.	Psalm 34:17
23. You will not be condemned.	If you take refuge in the Lord.	Psalm 34:22
24. You will have your heart's desire.	If you delight in the Lord.	Psalm 37:4
25. You will enjoy great peace.	If you are meek.	Psalm 37:11
26. The Lord will uphold you.	If you are righteous.	Psalm 37:17
27. Your feet will not slip.	If God's law is in your heart.	Psalm 37:31
28. The Lord will deliver you.	If you take refuge in him.	Psalm 37:40
29. God will make you into a leader.	If you love righteousness.	Psalm 45: 7
30. God will help you in trouble.	If God is your refuge and strength.	Psalm 46:1
31. God will be your guide until death.	If he is your God.	Psalm 48:14
32. God will accept your worship.	If you are broken-hearted.	Psalm 50:17
33. The Lord will sustain you.	If you cast your burden on him.	Psalm 55:22
34. You will not fear people.	If your trust is in God.	Psalm 56:11
35. God will fill your mouth.	If you open it wide.	Psalm 81:10
36. No good thing will be withheld from you.	If you are blameless.	Psalm 84:11
37. You will not be afraid at night.	If you rest under God's shadow.	Psalm 91:5
38. You will be taught from God's law.	If you accept God's discipline.	Psalm 94:12
39. The Lord will remove your transgressions.	If you fear the Lord.	Psalm 103:11
40. You will experience God's everlasting love.	If you fear him.	Psalm 103:17
41. You will not fear bad news.	If your heart is steadfast.	Psalm 112:7
42. You will lead a pure life.	If you live by God's word.	Psalm 119:9
43. You will survive affliction.	If you delight in God's law.	Psalm 119:92
44. You will experience great peace.	If you love God's law.	Psalm 119:165
45. The Lord will watch over your life.	If you trust in the Lord.	Psalm 121:7
46. You will endure and not be shaken.	If you trust in the Lord.	Psalm 125:1
47. The Lord will give you sleep.	If you love him.	Psalm 127:2
48. The Lord is near to you.	When you call on him in truth.	Psalm 145:18
49. The Lord delights in you.	When you are humble.	Psalm 149:4

Martin Luther and promises

The promises of the devil and the promises of God

"If God promises something, then faith must fight a long and bitter fight, for reason concludes that God's promises are impossible. Therefore faith must battle against reason and its doubts. The devil, too, approaches us with promises, that seem to be very plausible. It certainly requires at times a keen mind to be able to distinguish between God's true and the devil's false promises. The promises of the devil seem to be very pleasant and acceptable. Faith is something that is busy, powerful and creative. It changes the mind and heart. While reason holds on to what is seen, faith apprehends the things that are not seen. Faith goes against our reason and sees invisible things as if they had already materialized. This explains why faith, unlike hearing is not found in many people. For only few believe, while the great majority cling to the things that are present and can be touched and handled rather than to the Word.

This, then, is the characteristic of the genuine divine promises, that they are contrary to reason so that reason refuses to believe them. The promises of the devil, on the other hand, are in full agreement with reason and are readily and uncritically accepted. God's promises which are true and faithful, lead to the cross, and by the cross to his eternal blessing. Therefore reason is offended by them in two ways.

Reason does not think about anything that is invisible and in the distant future, and it detests the cross as it views the cross as a calamity that is everlasting and has no end. That is the reason why despite the wealth of the divine promises, few people believe them. But those who do believe God's promises are those whose hearts are led by the Holy Spirit so that, like Abraham, they defy all foes and cling to the Word of God who calls them.

Before Abraham came to Canaan he was blessed in many ways, but in the land of promise, he, despite his strong faith was forced to go into another country to escape the ravages of famine. God does this on purpose to test the faith of his saints. However, after a short time, God restores to them not only earthly prosperity, as Abraham became very wealthy, but God also gives them a greater faith and a deeper experience of his divine grace and mercy. For this reason Paul says in Romans 5:3 that though God's saints sigh under their cross, yet they glory in their tribulations when they discover how wonderfully God directs their life. God thus proves himself to be the Protector of all who put their trust in him. He tests their faith, but never forsakes them. Finally, he gloriously delivers them and at the same time blesses others with them." *Martin Luther*

The promises of God

Our thinking: It's impossible
God's promise: All things are possible
(Luke 18:27)
Our thinking: "I'm too tired"
God's promise: 1 will give you rest
(Matthew 11:28-30)
Our thinking: "Nobody really loves me"
God's promise: 1 love you (John 3:16;
John 13:34)
Our thinking: "1 can't go on"
God's promise: My grace is sufficient
(2 Corinthians 12:9; Psalm 91:15)
Our thinking: "I can't figure things out"
God's promise: I will direct your steps
(Proverbs 3:5, 6)
Our thinking: "I can't do it"
God's promise: You can do all things
(Philippians 4:13)
Our thinking: "I'm not able"
God's promise: I am able
(2 Corinthians 9:8)
Our thinking: "It's not worth it"
God's promise: It will be worth it

(Romans 8:28)
Our thinking: "I can't forgive myself"
God's promise: I forgive you
(1 John 1:9; Romans 8:1)
Our thinking: "I can't manage"
God's promise: I will supply all your
needs (Philippians 4:19)
Our thinking: "I'm afraid"
God's promise: I have not given you a
spirit of fear (2 Timothy 1:7)
Our thinking: "I'm always worried and
frustrated"
God's promise: Cast all your cares on
me (1 Peter 5:7)
Our thinking: "I don't have enough faith"
God's promise: I've given everyone a
measure of faith (Romans 12:3)
Our thinking: "I'm not smart enough"
God's promise: I give you wisdom
(1 Corinthians 1:30)
Our thinking: "I feel all alone"
God's promise: I will never leave you
or forsake you (Hebrews 13:5)
Author unknown

Applying New Testament promises to daily living

The variety of New Testament promises

In the New Testament there are a wealth of promises. Many of these promises do have conditions attached to them. But this first list are unconditional promises.

Unconditional promises and statements

1. Jesus' yoke is light: Matthew 1:30.
2. All things are possible with God: Matthew 19:26
3. Jesus has all authority in heaven and on earth: Matthew 28:18.
4. God does not show favoritism: Acts 10:34
5. Everyone will have to give an account of himself before God: Romans 14:12.
6. There is freedom where the Spirit of the Lord is: 2 Corinthians 3:17.
7. Godly sorrow brings repentance which leads to salvation: 2 Corinthians 7:10.
8. In Christ there is no Greek or Jew: Colossians 3:11.
9. Jesus remains faithful to us, even when we are unfaithful to him: 2 Timothy 2:13.
10. The Lord knows those who are his: 2 Timothy 2:19.
11. Jesus never changes: he is the same yesterday, today, and forever: Hebrews 13:8.
12. God never tempts us: James 1:13.
13. Every good gift comes from the Father: James 1:17.
14. Jesus is now in heaven at the right hand (of power) of the Father: 1 Peter 3:22.

15. When Jesus comes again everybody will see him: Revelation 1:7.

New Testament promises about spiritual blessings

The two most common reasons for not enjoying all the amazing spiritual blessings which are promised in the New Testament are:

- our **ignorance**. We just do not know what these blessings are.
- our **laziness** in not claiming them. We are not spiritually thirsting and hungering after them in the way that we should be.

1. THE GOSPELS		
The promise	*The condition*	*The reference*
1. We can experience the kingdom of heaven.	If we are poor in spirit.	Matthew 5:3
2. We can be full of God's righteousness.	If we hunger and thirst for this.	Matthew 5:8
3. We will see God.	If we are pure in heart.	Matthew 5:8
4. We will be called God's children.	If we act as peace-makers.	Matthew 5:9
5. We will find spiritual refreshment.	If we wear Jesus' yoke.	Matthew 11:29
6. We can enter the kingdom of heaven.	If we are like little children.	Matthew 18:3
7. We will be the greatest in the kingdom.	If we are humble as a child.	Matthew 18:4
8. We will receive what we ask for.	Where two or three pray together in Jesus' name.	Matthew 18:20
9. We will be saved.	If we endure to the end.	Matthew 24:13
10. Jesus will be with us until the end of the age.	If we teach and baptize.	Matthew 28:19
11. We will not be judged.	If we don't judge others.	Luke 6:37
12. We will not be condemned.	If we don't condemn others.	Luke 6:37
13. We will be forgiven.	Provided that we forgive.	Luke 6:37
14. We will be given the Holy Spirit.	If we ask the Father for this.	Luke 11:13
15. We may have eternal life.	If we believe in Jesus.	John 3:16
16. We may have eternal life.	If we eat Jesus' flesh and drink his blood.	John 6:54
17. We will know and be set free by the truth.	If we hold to Jesus' teaching.	John 8:31, 32
18. We will do greater works than Jesus did.	If we believe in Jesus.	John 14:12
19. The Holy Spirit will be with us forever.	If we obey Jesus.	John 14:15, 16
20. We will be loved by the Father.	If we keep Jesus' commands.	John 14:21
21. We will be fruitful.	If we abide in Jesus.	John 15:5
22. We are Jesus' friends.	If we obey him.	John 15:14

2. THE ACTS		
The promise	*The condition*	*The reference*
1. We will receive power.	After the Holy Spirit has come on us.	Acts 1:8
2. We will be forgiven our sins.	If we believe in Jesus.	Acts 10:43

3. THE LETTERS FROM ROMANS TO 2 PETER		
The promise	*The condition*	*The reference*
1. We are no longer condemned.	Provided that we are in Jesus.	Romans 8:1
2. Our bodies will come alive after death.	If Jesus' Spirit is in us.	Romans 8:11
3. We are God's children.	So long as we are led by the Spirit.	Romans 8:14
4. We are co-heirs with Jesus.	Provided we are God's children.	Romans 8:17
5. We are more than conquerors.	If we abide in Jesus' love.	Romans 8:37
6. Jesus is the end of the law.	So long as we believe in him.	Romans 10:4
7. We will be saved.	So long as we bear witness to Jesus.	Romans 10:9
8. Jesus is our wisdom from God	So long as we are in Jesus.	1 Corinthians 1:30
9. Jesus is our righteousness.	So long as we are in Jesus.	1 Corinthians 1:30
10. Jesus is our holiness.	So long as we are in Jesus.	1 Corinthians 1:30
11. Jesus is our redemption.	So long as we are in Jesus.	1 Corinthians 1:30
12. We have the spirit of understanding.	If we are open to the Spirit.	1 Corinthians 2:12
13. We need not work in vain.	Provided that we work in the Lord.	1 Corinthians 15:58
14. We can be new creations.	If we are in Jesus.	2 Corinthians 5:17
15. We can knock over spiritual strongholds.	Through God's divine power.	2 Corinthians 10:4
16. We are justified.	By faith in Jesus.	Galatians 2:16
17. We are clothed with Jesus.	If we are baptized into Jesus.	Galatians 3:27
18. We are Abraham's seed.	If we are Jesus'.	Galatians 3:29
19. We will not gratify sinful desires.	If we walk in the Spirit.	Galatians 5:16

20. We are no longer under the law.	If we are led by the Spirit.	Galatians 5:18
21. We will reap a spiritual harvest.	If we don't give up.	Galatians 6:9
22. We are sealed with the Holy Spirit.	If we believe in Jesus.	Ephesians 1:13
23. We have access to the Father by the Spirit.	Through Jesus.	Ephesians 2:18
24. Our hearts will be kept by God's peace.	If we pray about everything.	Philippians 4:6, 7
25. We will be blameless.	If we continue in our faith.	Colossians 1:21-23
26. We will live with Jesus.	If we have died with him.	2 Timothy 2:11
27. We will reign with Jesus.	If we endure.	2 Timothy 2:12
28. We are equipped for every good work.	By the Scripture.	2 Timothy 3:16
29. We may receive mercy and grace.	By approaching God's throne of grace.	Hebrews 4:16
30. We will be completely saved.	If we come to God through Jesus.	Hebrews 7:25
31. We will be made perfect.	If we have been made holy.	Hebrews 10:14
32. We will receive what God has promised.	If we persevere.	Hebrews 10:36
33. We can please God.	With faith.	Hebrews 11:6
34. We will be rewarded by God.	If we seek him earnestly.	Hebrews 11:6
35. God treats us like his sons.	If we are disciplined by him.	Hebrews 12:7
36. God gives grace.	To the humble.	James 4:6
37. God draws near to us.	If we draw near to him.	James 4:8
38. We are shielded by God's power.	Through faith.	1 Peter 1:5
39. God is attentive to our prayers.	So long as we are righteous.	1 Peter 3:12
40. We will be blessed.	Even if we are insulted for the sake of Jesus.	1 Peter 4:14
41. We will receive grace.	So long as we are humble and not proud.	1 Peter 5:5
42. We will never fall.	If we make our election sure.	2 Peter 1:10
43. The Lord will deliver us from trials.	If we are godly.	2 Peter 2:9

4. THE LETTERS OF JOHN AND THE BOOK OF REVELATION

	The promise	The condition	The reference
1.	We have fellowship with other Christians.	So long as we walk in the light.	1 John 1:7
2.	God will forgive us our sins.	If we confess them to him.	1 John 1:9
3.	We will be aware that we know Jesus.	If we obey his commands.	1 John 2:3
4.	God's love is completed in us.	If we obey his word.	1 John 2:5
5.	We will not make a brother stumble.	If we live in the light.	1 John 2:10
6.	We need nobody else to teach us.	If God's anointing remains in us.	1 John 2:27
7.	We have confidence before God.	If our hearts do not condemn us.	1 John 3:21
8.	We know that Jesus lives in us.	By the Spirit he gave us.	1 John 3:24
9.	God's love is made perfect in us.	If we love one another.	1 John 4:12
10.	God lives in us.	If we acknowledge that Jesus is God's Son.	1 John 4:15
11.	We live in God and God lives in us.	If we love.	1 John 4:16
12.	We are born of God.	If we believe that Jesus is the Christ.	1 John 5:1
13.	We know that we love God's	When we love and obey God. children.	1 John 5:2
14.	We overcome the world.	If we are born of God.	1 John 5:4
15.	We have eternal life.	If we have life in Jesus.	1 John 5:11
16.	We have both Jesus and the Father.	If we continue in Christian teaching.	2 John 9
17.	We will be kept in the hour of trial.	If we endure patiently.	Revelation 3:10
18.	Jesus will come into our lives.	If we open the door to him.	Revelation 3:20
19	We can overcome the accuser.	By the blood of the Lamb.	Revelation 12:10, 11

New Testament warnings to heed
God has taken infinite care to surround us with wholesome Christian teaching in the Bible so that we can take great strides in the Christian life. And to keep us on the straight and narrow God has provided us with a number of timely warnings in the New Testament.

WARNINGS		
The warning	*The condition*	*The reference*
1. Jesus will deny us.	If we deny him.	2 Timothy 2:12
2. You will go through persecution.	If you lead a godly life.	2 Timothy 3:12
3. No sacrifice for sins is left.	If we keep on deliberately sinning.	Hebrews 10:26
4. We are guilty of breaking all of God's commands.	If we just break one of them.	James 2:10
5. We do not have.	Because we do not ask God.	James 4:2
6. Our prayers are unanswered.	Because we ask with wrong motives.	James 4:3
7. We deceive ourselves.	If we say we have not sinned.	1 John 1:8
8. We walk in darkness.	If we hate a fellow-Christian.	1 John 2:11
9. The love of the Father is not in us.	If we love the world.	1 John 2:15
10. Anyone who denies that Jesus is the Christ.	Is a liar.	1 John 2:22
11. Anyone who worships the beast.	Will not find his name in the book of life.	Revelation 13:8
12. People will be thrown into the lake of fire.	If their names are not in the book of life.	Revelation 20:15

Christian discipleship

Learners

It's been said that Christians should stick large "L"s on their front and back, like a person learning to drive a car has to have "L" plates to warn all other car drivers about their inability to drive properly. A good definition of a Christian disciple would be: "Someone who is learning to be like Jesus."

Seven qualifications for Christian discipleship

1. You must be born again: John 3:1-8.
2. You must confess with your mouth that "Jesus is Lord" Romans 10:9.
3. You must do the deeds that God has planned for you to do: Ephesians 2:10.

4. You must be prepared that this may divide your family right down the middle: Matthew 10:34-37.
5. You must have an increasing love for fellow-Christians: John 13:35.
6. You must never let go of Jesus' teaching: John 8:31-32.
7. You must abide in Jesus: John 15:7-8.

The worldly view and the Christian view

As disciples of Jesus we have a completely different way of viewing things. What the world might count on Christians may set very little store by. What Christians may think as essential worldly people may totally disregard.

Seven worldly certainties

1. Beauty

Charm is deceptive and beauty is fleeting: Proverbs 31:30.

2. Promises made by humans

Don't put your trust in anyone, not even in powerful people: Psalm 146:3.

3. Riches

One problem with riches is that they are here today and gone tomorrow. Even though worldly people know this, they still put their trust in them, and spend their whole working lives in the pursuit of becoming rich. See Proverbs 23:5.

4. The future

Don't boast about tomorrow, for nobody knows what tomorrow will bring: Proverbs 27:1.

5. Friendships

The closest of human friendships cannot compare with our friendship with Jesus: John 16:32.

6. Life is everything

The problem with this view is that it is just not true. The one certainty in life is its uncertainty. See James 4:14.

7. Worldly glory

Worldly glory is a mirage, and only a temporary one at that. See 1 Peter 2:24.

Seven comforting certainties

1.God's promises

None of God's promises have ever failed: I Kings 8:56.

2. Foundations that can be relied on

The Christian's sure foundation is Jesus: Isaiah 28:16.

3. A certain reward

A Christian's reward may come mostly in the after life, but it is assured: Matthew 10:42.

4. Accepted by God

There is nothing on earth that can compare with this: John 6:37.

5. God's love

Christians are aware that by this world's standards they may have very little and may even have to go through terrible persecution. But Christians believe that absolutely nothing can separate them from God's love. See Romans 8:38-39.

6. Immortality is assured

"What will happen to me when I die?" Christians and non-Christians give completely different answers to this question. If you told a non-Christian that you are looking forward to "an eternal house in heaven" you would probably just receive a disbelieving smile. See 2 Corinthians 5:1.

7. An eternal anchor

Christians are taught that they should be like pilgrims passing through this world. Their focus is heaven, and so they have this eternal anchor. See Hebrews 6:19.

Pride comes before a fall

No matter how young or how old, or how experienced or how inexperienced a Christian may be, we are never free of being tempted to be proud. Pride is a sin we cannot be too much on our guard against. Pride is linked to all sorts of unsavory characteristics:

- Pride is linked with violence: Psalm 73:6.
- Pride is linked with scheming devices: Psalm 10:2.
- Pride is linked with a haughty spirit: Proverbs 16:18.
- Pride is linked with haughty eyes: Proverbs 21:4.
- Pride is linked with lustful eyes and boasting: 1 John 2:16.

How to "abide" in Jesus

John 15

One of the quickest ways to know what "abiding" in Jesus means is to read John 15:1-7 everyday for a month. You could write out those particular verses or parts of verses which hit you as you read the passage. Just five are listed below:

- Remain in the vine: John 15:4.
- Apart from the vine we can to nothing: John 15:5.
- The opposite to abiding in Jesus is too terrible to contemplate: John 15:6.
- Jesus' words must be in us: John 15:7.
- Obedience plays a key part in abiding: John 15:10.

Focus on God's presence

In the Old Testament the Lord God promised to be with his people:

Even though Jacob had been so deceitful to his father, God, in his great mercy, promised to be with him: Genesis 28:15. See also Genesis 31:3; Exodus 3:12; 29:45.

After the dreadful incident of the people of Israel making a golden calf and worshiping it, God greatly encouraged Moses with this promise: "My presence will go with you, and I will give you rest" Exodus 33:14. See also Leviticus 26:12.

Sometimes it feels as if every day is a spiritual battle. The promise made about war in Deuteronomy 20:1 can be applied to the battles we face in life. The promise points out that just as God had been with his people during the Exodus, so he would be with them now in the impending battle.

Christians may feel that they are

prepared for trials. However, when they come, the one thing we need above all else is God's presence. Isaiah has a wonderful promise about God promising to be with us, whether we are passing through turbulent waters or through raging fire: Isaiah 43:2. See also Zechariah 2:10.

Have some spiritual heroes

It's a good idea to have in mind some godly people whom you can look up to and can see how they managed to become spiritually strong and so were effective in their service for God.

1. Samuel

There are two people in the Bible about whom it is said that they grew in favor with God and with men. One of these people was the boy Samuel: 1 Samuel 2:26. The other person was Jesus. When he went back with Mary and Joseph to Nazareth as a 12-year-old, Luke records that, "Jesus grew in wisdom and stature, and in favor with God and men" Luke 2:52.

2. John the Baptist

If we had come across John the Baptist in the Old Testament we would not have thought that he was out of place. Luke says of the outspoken, fearless prophet: he "grew and became strong in spirit" Luke 1:80.

3. Paul the apostle

After his dramatic conversion experience on the Damascus Road Paul did not take life easy. He launched into a one man preaching campaign, telling the Jews in Damascus that Jesus really was the long-awaited Messiah. This, according to Luke, happened because Paul "grew more and more powerful" Acts 9:22.

4. The Christians at Thessalonica

Paul wrote his letters to different churches to teach them about the things they asked him and about any wrong paths he heard that they were taking. About the young, vibrant Christians at Thessalonica Paul had much to praise. He singles out two reasons why they were making such good progress:

- Their **faith in Jesus** was growing more and more: 2 Thessalonians 1:3.
- The **love** they had for **each other** was increasing: 2 Thessalonians 1:3.

On to maturity

Spiritual maturity should be the goal and experience of every Christian. Too many Christians are quite content to remain spiritual babies. See 1 Corinthians 13:11; 1 Corinthians 14:20; Hebrews 5:14.

Overcoming temptation is a sign of spiritual maturity: 1 John 2:14.

Knowledge of Jesus is another sign of spiritual maturity. Ephesians 4:13 contains this word "maturity." "...until we all reach unity in the faith and in the knowledge of the Son of God and become *mature*, attaining to the whole measure of the fullness of Christ."

3 PRAYER

Introduction

"Prayer is the single most important way to grow in the Christian life." Many Christians would immediately agree with this statement, but know that their own prayer life is very weak and so wonder how they can remedy this.

To help you find out for yourself what the Bible really teaches about prayer, chapter 3 examines the prayers of Jesus, as well as Jesus' teaching on prayer. It also focuses attention on some of the prayers in the greatest Old Testament book about prayer, the Psalms. There is also a study on the teaching Paul gave about prayer in his letters. The final pages of chapter 3 give an Internet site where you can hear Christian hymns and dozens of classic Christian prayers to choose from to enhance your own prayer life.

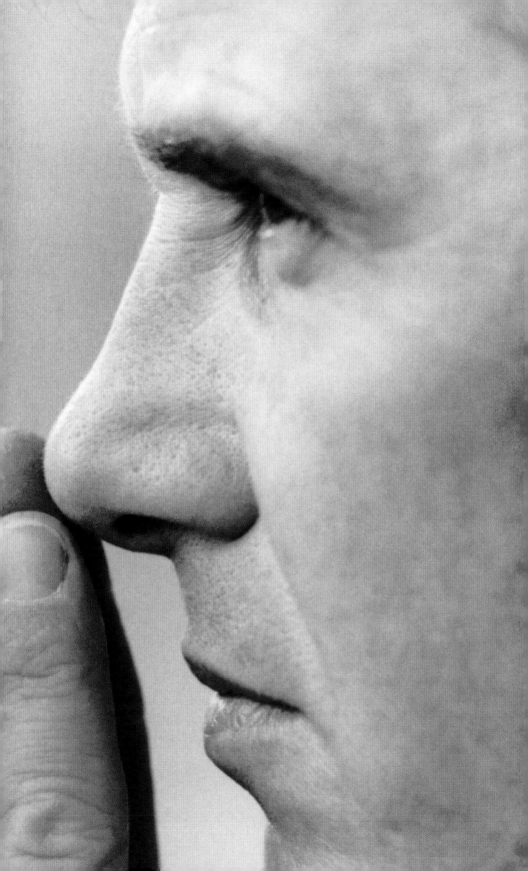

Getting started

Many people find that the most difficult thing about prayer is getting started. The way to overcome this is to reflect on a "draw near to God" verse.

Draw near to God verses

Choose one of the following verses as you begin to pray.

1. **It is good to be near God.** See Psalm 73:28.
2. **We draw near to God.** See Hebrews 7:19.
3. **Let us draw near to God.** See Hebrews 10:22.
4. **Come near to God.** James 4:8.

In James 4:8 there is a wonderful promise to claim. As we seek to draw near to God, so he promises that he will draw near to us.

Try praying another person's prayer

Martin Luther used the following two prayers with his own family. They illustrate how a father should teach his household to conduct morning and evening devotions.

Morning Devotions

As soon as you get out of bed in the morning, you should say:

May the will of God, the Father, the Son and the Holy Spirit be done! Amen.

Then, kneeling or standing, say the creed and pray the Lord's Prayer. If you wish, you may then pray this little prayer as well:

My Heavenly Father, I thank you, through Jesus Christ, your beloved Son, that you kept me safe from all evil and danger last night. Save me, I pray, today as well, from every evil and sin, so that all I do and the way that I live will please you. I put myself in your care, body and soul and all that I have. Let your presence be with me, so that the evil enemy will not gain power over me. Amen.

After that, with joy go about your work and perhaps sing a song inspired by the Ten Commandments or your own thoughts.

Evening Devotions

When you go to bed in the evening, you should say:

May the will of God, the Father, the Son and the

Holy Spirit be done! Amen.

Then, kneeling or standing, say the creed and pray the Lord's Prayer.

If you wish, then you may pray this little prayer as well:

My Heavenly Father, I thank you, through Jesus Christ, your beloved Son, that you have protected me, by your grace. Forgive, I pray, all my sins and the evil I have done. Protect me, by your grace, tonight. I put myself in your care, body and soul and all that I have. Let your presence be with me, so that the evil enemy will not gain power over me. Amen.

After this, go to sleep immediately with joy. *Luther's Little Instruction Book*

Being blessed by the ten Bible benedictions

1. Numbers 6:24-26
2. Romans 1:7
3. Romans 15:33
4. Romans 16:24
5. Ephesians 6:23, 24
6. 2 Thessalonians 3:16
7. 1 Timothy 1:2
8. 2 Timothy 4:22
9. 1 Peter 5:14
10. 2 Peter 1:2

Something to do

Look up the above ten blessings found in the Bible.

Note what blessing the author of each prayer is praying will be received by the person listening to the prayer, or reading

the prayer.

Then reflect on the truth of the following words of Augustine: "God is more anxious to bestow his blessings on us than we are to receive them."

Compose a prayer of your own in which you ask for some specific blessing from God to be on a person who is close to you.

Learning from the prayers of Jesus

The priority of prayer

We are all agreed about the importance of prayer. There are more Christian books written on this topic than on any other subject. Yet, if we are honest with ourselves, prayer is often our Achilles' heel. For while we know in theory about how crucial it is, in practice we often feel like total failures!

This need not be the case. This does not have to continue. The next few pages give some very practical studies which are designed to kick-start a prayer life that may have seen better days, and encourage our prayer lives – no matter what state of repair or disrepair they may be in.

New Testament prayers

Over the next six pages have a go at reading and learning from the following New Testament prayers. Each time you have studied one of the prayers have a time of prayer. Pray about what you have learned.

Prayers linked to Jesus
1. The prayer of the heavenly host

> Glory to God in the highest heaven,
>   and on earth peace among those
>   whom he favors! *Luke 2:14 NRSV*

This is the prayer that the shepherds heard in the fields. It announced the birth of Jesus to them. So the shepherds went to find the baby Jesus. Because of its opening words it is also known as the *Gloria in excelsis*.

Something to do

Write out a prayer praising God for the birth of Jesus.

2. The Lord's Prayer

> Our Father in heaven,
> hallowed be your name.
> Your kingdom come.
> Your will be done,
>   on earth as it is in heaven.
> Give us this day our daily bread.
> And forgive us our debts,
>   as we also have forgiven our debtors.
> And do not bring us to the time of
>   trial,but rescue us from the evil one.
> *Matthew 6:9-13, NRSV*

This prayer is so familiar to us that we are in danger of overlooking it, or never concentrating when it is prayed.

Something to do

Read the comments of Francis of Assisi below. Then make up your own one sentence prayer on each of the petitions of the Lord's Prayer. Write each one down and use it as a prayer.

The Lord's Prayer explained
Our Father

Our Father, most holy, our Creator, Redeemer, Savior and Comforter.

Who art in heaven

May your kingdom shine in us so that we may know the greatness of your benefits, the breadth of your promises, the height of your majesty, and the depth of your judgments (see Ephesians 3:18).

Hallowed be thy name
May I have your grace to reverence your name in all I think, in all I say, and in all I do, throughout this day.

Thy kingdom come
May your kingdom so come into our hearts that you may reign in us by your grace and enable us to enter your kingdom, where you are clearly seen, and where we enjoy you forever.

Thy will be done in earth as it is in heaven
How we love you with all our heart, as we are always thinking about you; with our souls we are always desiring you; with all our minds we direct all our thoughts towards you. We seek your honor in everything. With all our strength we submit our faculties to you. All our spirits and bodies we submit to only obeying your love. We will love our neighbors as ourselves. We will do our utmost to encourage the whole world to love you. We rejoice with those who rejoice as if the happy moment had been our own. We sympathize with the sad and never offend anyone.

Give us this day our daily bread
Our Lord Jesus Christ, your dear Son, reminds us of and makes us understand the love he has for us. He makes us love all that he has said, done, and suffered for us.

And forgive us our trespasses
We are forgiven through your great mercy and because of the passion of your dear Son our Lord Jesus Christ.

As we forgive them that trespass against us
Grant, O Lord, that even though we do not completely forgive we may nevertheless be completely forgiven. May we truly love our enemies for your sake; may we pray sincerely to you for them and may we repay no one evil for evil. May we strive to be useful to everyone for your sake.

And lead us not into temptation
Lead us not into hidden or open temptation, or sudden or persistent temptations.

But deliver us from evil
Deliver us from past evil, present evil, and future evil. Amen. *Francis of Assisi, Rule*

prayers found in Luke's Gospel, which have been called "poem prayers."

The *Magnificat*

My soul doth magnify the Lord : and my spirit hath rejoiced in God my Savior.

For he hath regarded : the lowliness of his handmaiden.

For behold, from henceforth : all generations shall call me blessed.

For he that is mighty hath magnified me : and holy is his Name.

And his mercy is on them that fear him : throughout all generations.

He hath showed strength with his arm : he hath scattered the proud in the imagination of their hearts.

He hath put down the mighty from their seat : and hath exalted the humble and meek.

He hath filled the hungry with good things : and the rich he hath sent empty away.

He remembering his mercy hath holpen his servant Israel : as he promised to our forefathers,

Abraham and his seed, for ever.

Magnificat, Luke 1:46-55, Book of Common Prayer

Variety is the spice of life

One problem that many Christians encounter in their prayer life is becoming stale. Sometimes it can be a help to read the prayers of the New Testament in a Bible version that you have never tried before or have not read for some time. You can try this with the following three

The *Benedictus*

Blessed be the Lord God of Israel : for he hath visited, and redeemed his people;

And hath raised up a mighty salvation for us : in the house of his servant David;

As he spake by the mouth of his holy
  Prophets : which have been since the
  world began;
That we should be saved from our
  enemies : and from the hands of all
  that hate us.
To perform the mercy promised to our
  forefathers : and to remember his
  holy Covenant;
To perform the oath which he sware to
  our forefather Abraham : that he
  would give us;
That we being delivered out of the
  hand of our enemies : might serve
  him without fear;
In holiness and righteousness before
  him : all the days of our life.
And thou, child, shalt be called the
  Prophet of the Highest : for thou
  shalt go before the face of the Lord
  to prepare his ways;
To give knowledge of salvation unto
  his people : for the remission of their
  sins,
Through the tender mercy of our God :
  whereby the day-spring from on
  high hath visited us;
To give light to them that sit in
  darkness, and in the shadow of
  death : and to guide our feet into the
  way of peace.
Glory be to the Father, and to the Son
  : and to the Holy Ghost;
As it was in the beginning, is now, and
  ever shall be : world without end.
  Amen.
  *Benedictus, Luke 1:68-79, The Book of
  Common Prayer*

The *Nunc Dimittis*
  Lord, now lettest thou thy servant
    depart in peace : according to thy word.
  For mine eyes have seen : thy salvation,
  Which thou hast prepared : before the
    face of all people;
  To be a light to lighten the Gentiles : and
    to be the glory of thy people Israel.
    *Nunc Dimittis, Luke 2:29-32, Book of
    Common Prayer*

Something to do
See who is praying each of the above
prayers and what led them to pray in the
way they did. These spontaneous songs
of praise captured the hearts of the early
Christians so that they used them
themselves to sing God's praises.

  Each of the names given to these
prayers is taken from the opening words
in the Latin translation. So

  • *Magnificat* translates, "My soul
    magnifies [glorifies] the Lord"
  • *Benedictus* translates the opening
    word, "Blessed"
  • *Nunc Dimittis* translates "Now, let...
    depart."
  • *Gloria in Excelsis* translates "Glory in
    the highest."

Look out for allusions to the New Testament
In the *Magnificat* compare Psalm 31:8
with the opening line, and also look for
an allusion to 1 Samuel 2:7.

  In the *Benedictus*, look for echoes from
Malachi 3:1; 7:20; and Jeremiah 11:5.

Four more prayers of Jesus

I thank you, Father, Lord of heaven and earth, because you have hidden these things from the wise and the intelligent and have revealed them to infants; yes, Father, for such was your gracious will. *Luke 10:21, NRSV*

Father, glorify your name. *John 12:28, NRSV*

Father, if you are willing, remove this cup from me; yet, not my will but yours be done. *Luke 22:42, NRSV*

Father, I thank you for having heard me. I knew that you always hear me, but I have said this for the sake of the crowd standing here, so that they may believe that you sent me. *John 11:41, 42, NRSV*

Something to do

Look up the context of the above four prayers.

The prayers of Jesus on the cross

Father, forgive them; for they know not what they do. *Luke 23:34, KJV*

My God, my God, why hast thou forsaken me? *Matthew 27:46, KJV*

It is finished. *John 19:30, KJV*

Father, into thy hands I commend my spirit. *Luke 23:46, KJV*

Something to do

Read the above four prayers and then meditate on what now follows.

Deny ourselves and imitate Christ through bearing the cross
The Voice of Christ

My child, the more you depart from yourself, the more you will be able to enter into me. As the giving up of exterior things brings inner peace, so the forsaking of self unites you to God. I will have you learn perfect surrender to my will, without contradiction or complaint.

Follow me. I am the Way, the Truth, and the Life. Without the Way, there is no going. Without the Truth, there is no knowing. Without the Life, there is no living. I am the Way which you must follow, the Truth which you must believe, the Life for which you must hope. I am the inviolable Way, the infallible Truth, the unending Life. I am the Way that is straight, the supreme Truth, the Life that is true, the blessed, the uncreated Life. If you abide in my Way you shall know the Truth, and the Truth shall make you free, and you shall attain life everlasting.

If you wish to enter into life, keep my commandments. If you will know the truth, believe in me. If you will be perfect, sell all. If you will be my disciple, deny yourself. If you will possess the blessed life, despise this present life. If you will be exalted in heaven, humble yourself on earth. If you wish to reign with me, carry the cross with me. For only the servants of the cross find the life of blessedness and of true light.

The Disciple

Lord Jesus, because your way is narrow and despised by the world, grant that I may despise the world and imitate you. For the servant is not greater than his Lord, nor the disciple above the Master.

Let your servant be trained in your life, for there is my salvation and true holiness. Whatever else I read or hear does not fully refresh or delight me.

The Voice of Christ

My child, now that you know these things and have read them all, happy will you be if you do them. He who has my commandments and keeps them, he it is that loves me. And I will love him and will show myself to him, and will bring it about that he will sit down with me in my Father's kingdom.

The Disciple

Lord Jesus, as you have said, so may it be, and what you have promised, let it be my lot to win. I have received the cross, from your hand I have received it. I will carry it, carry it even to death as you have laid it on me. Truly, the life of a good man is a cross, but it leads to heaven. We have begun – we may not go back.

Take courage, brethren, let us go forward together and Jesus will be with us. For Jesus' sake we have taken this cross. For Jesus' sake let us persevere with it. He will be our help as he is also our leader and guide. Behold, our King goes before us and will fight for us. Let us follow him. Let no one be afraid. Let us be prepared to meet death valiantly in battle. Let us not allow our glory to be blemished by running away from the cross. *The Imitation of Christ, ascribed to Thomas à Kempis*

Learning from other New Testament prayers

And now, Lord, look at their threats, and grant to your servants to speak your word with all boldness, while you stretch out your hand to heal, and signs and wonders are performed through the name of your holy servant Jesus. *Acts 4:29, 30, NRSV*

Lord Jesus, receive my spirit...Lord, do not hold this sin against them. *Stephen, as he was being martyred. Acts 7:59, 60, NRSV*

Now may the God of peace, who brought back from the dead our Lord Jesus, the great shepherd of the sheep, by the blood of the eternal covenant, make you complete in everything good so that you may

do his will, working among us that which is pleasing in his sight, through Jesus Christ, to whom be the glory for ever and ever. Amen. *Hebrews 13:20, 21, NRSV*

Blessed be the God and Father of our Lord Jesus Christ! By his great mercy we have been born anew to a living hope through the resurrection of Jesus Christ from the dead, and to an inheritance which is imperishable, undefiled, and unfading, kept in heaven for you, who by God's power are guarded through faith for a salvation ready to be revealed in the last time. *1 Peter 1:3-5, NRSV*

Now to him who is able to keep you from falling, and to make you stand without blemish in the presence of his glory with rejoicing, to the only God our Savior, through Jesus Christ our Lord, be glory, majesty, power, and authority, before all time and now and for ever. Amen. *Jude 24, 25, NRSV*

To him who loves us and freed us from our sins by his blood, and made us to be a kingdom, priests serving his God and Father, to him be glory and dominion for ever and ever. Amen. *Revelation 1:5, 6, NRSV*

You are worthy, our Lord and God, to receive glory and honor and

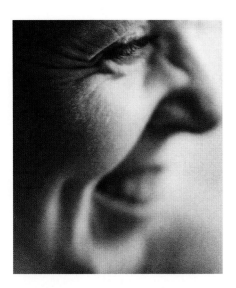

power, for you created all things,
and by your will they existed and
were created. *Revelation 4:11, NRSV*

Amen! Blessing and glory and wisdom
and thanksgiving and honor
and power and might
be to our God for ever and ever!
Amen. *Revelation 7:12, NRSV*

Great and amazing are your deeds,
Lord God the Almighty!
Just and true are your ways,
King of the nations!
Lord, who will not fear
and glorify your name?
For you alone are holy.
All nations will come
and worship before you.
for your judgments have been
revealed. *Revelation 15:3, 4, NRSV*

Something to do

From the first five of the above prayers
find something in each one which
encourages you, and then thank God
for it.

From the last four of the above
prayers, all from the book of Revelation,
note something that each of them says
about God, and then make their words
of praise your own.

Prayer and meditation

"God knows all things. He knows what
we wish even before we ask for it. Yet
we must pray, for many reasons. But
first because Christ set us an example:
he went up into the mountains alone at
night to pray. And also because the
apostles tell us to pray: 'Pray
continually' (1 Thessalonians 5:17), and
men ought always to pray and not give
up (see Luke 18:1). But we ought to
pray to acquire grace for this life and
glory in the next. So we are told, 'For
everyone who asks receives; he who
seeks finds; and to him who knocks,
the door will be opened' (Luke 11:10).

We should also pray because in
constant prayer the soul is ignited with
the fire of divine love. Our Lord speaks
truly through the prophet, 'Is not my
word like fire…and like a hammer that
breaks a rock in pieces?' (Jeremiah
23:29). And the psalmist says, 'Your
speech is a burning fire' (Psalm 119:140
Vulgate)." *Richard Rolle, The Fire of Love*

Christian meditation in the Psalms

Something to do

For the next month try reading one psalm a day. You could start with the psalms that are found in the following four pages.

Then you could move on to read one psalm from the following classification of prayers in the Psalms.

Prayers to pray from the Psalms

1. Devotional prayers

  a. Penitence: Psalms 6; 32; 38; 51; 130; 143.
  b. Commitment to God: Psalms 3; 26; 27; 31; 54; 56; 57; 61; 62; 71; 86; 123; 131.
  c. In times of crisis: Psalms 4: 5; 11; 28; 41; 55; 59; 64; 70; 109; 120; 140; 141; 142.

2. Prayers of praise

  a. For God's providential care: Psalms 34; 35; 87; 91; 100; 107; 117; 121; 145; 145.
  b. For who God is: Psalms 19; 29; 33; 47; 50; 76; 93; 95; 96; 99; 104; 111; 113; 114; 115; 134; 139; 147; 148; 150.

3. Prayers of thanksgiving

  a. For specific mercies: 9; 30; 75; 103; 108; 116; 138; 144.
  b. For general mercies: 46; 48; 65; 66; 68; 81; 85; 98; 124; 126; 135; 136; 140.

Psalms to meditate on

You show me the path of life.
In your presence there is fullness
    of joy;
in your right hand are pleasures
    for evermore. *Psalm 16:11, NRSV*

I love you, O Lord, my strength.
    Psalm 18:1, NRSV

The Lord is my shepherd, I shall
    not want.
He makes me lie down in green
    pastures;
he leads me beside still waters;
    he restores my soul.
He leads me in right paths for his
    name's sake.
Even though I walk through the
    darkest valley, I fear no evil;
for you are with me;
    your rod and your staff –
    they comfort me.
You prepare a table before me
    in the presence of my enemies;
you anoint my head with oil;
    my cup overflows.
Surely goodness and mercy shall
    follow me all the days of my life,
and I shall dwell in the house of
    the Lord my whole life long.
    Psalm 23, NRSV

To you, O Lord, I lift up my soul.
...Make me to know your ways, O
   Lord; teach me your paths.
Lead me in your truth, and teach me,
   for you are the God of my salvation;
   for you I wait all day long.
Be mindful of your mercy, O Lord,
   and of your steadfast love,
   for they have been from of old.
   Psalm 25:1, 4-6, NRSV

The Lord is my light and my salvation;
   whom shall I fear?
The Lord is the stronghold of my life;
   of whom shall I be afraid?
...I believe that I shall see the
   goodness of the Lord in the land
   of the living.
Wait for the Lord;
   be strong, and let your heart
   take courage; wait for the Lord!
   Psalm 27:1, 13, 14, NRSV

For with you is the fountain of life;
   in your light we see light.
   Psalm 36:9, NRSV

Why are you cast down, O my soul,
   and why are you disquieted
   within me?
Hope in God; for I shall again praise
   him, my help and my God.
   Psalm 42:11, NRSV

Be still and know that I am God.
   Psalm 46:10, NRSV

Be merciful to me, O God, be merciful
   to me, for in you my soul takes
   refuge;
in the shadow of your wings I will
   take refuge, until the destroying
   storms pass by. *Psalm 57:1, NRSV*

Hear my cry, O God;
   listen to my prayer.
From the end of the earth I call to you,
   when my heart is faint.
Lead me to the rock
   that is higher than I;
for you are my refuge,
   a strong tower against the enemy.
   Psalm 61:1-3, NRSV

O God, you are my God, I seek you,
   my soul thirsts for you;
my flesh faints for you,
   as in a dry and weary land where
   there is no water. *Psalm 63:1, NRSV*

God be merciful unto us, and bless us :
and shew us the light of his
countenance, and be merciful unto us :
That thy way may be known upon
earth : thy saving health among all
nations.
Let the people praise thee, O God :
yea, let all the people praise thee.
O let the nations rejoice and be glad :
for thou shalt judge the folk
righteously, and govern the nations
upon earth.
Let the people praise thee, O God :
yea, let all the people praise thee.
Then shall the earth bring forth her
increase : and God, even our own
God, shall give us his blessing.
God shall bless us : and all the ends
of the world shall fear him.
*Deus misereatur, Psalm 67, Book of
Common Prayer*

Praise the Lord upon the harp : sing to
the harp with a psalm of thanksgiving.
With trumpets also and shawms : O
shew yourselves joyful before the
Lord the King.
Let the sea make a noise, and all that
therein is : the round world, and
they that dwell therein.
Let the floods clap their hands, and let
the hills be joyful together before the
Lord : for he cometh to judge the
earth.
With righteousness shall he judge the
world : and the people with equity.
*Cantate Domino, Psalm 98, Book of
Common Prayer*

How lovely is your dwelling-place,
O Lord of hosts!
My soul longs, indeed it faints
for the courts of the Lord;
my heart and my flesh sing for joy
to the living God.
Even the sparrow finds a home,
and the swallow a nest for herself,
where she may lay her young,
at your altars, O Lord of hosts,
my King and my God.
Happy are those who live in your
house, ever singing your praise.
Happy are those whose strength is in
you, in whose heart are the
highways of Zion.
As they go through the valley of Baca
they make it a place of springs;
the early rain also covers it with
pools.
They go from strength to strength;
the God of gods will be seen in Zion.
Psalm 84:1-7, NRSV

O sing unto the Lord a new song : for
   he hath done marvelous things.
With his own right hand, and with his
   holy arm : hath he gotten himself
   the victory.
The Lord declared his salvation : his
   righteousness hath he openly
   showed in the sight of the heathen.
He hath remembered his mercy and
   truth toward the house of Israel :
   and all the ends of the world have
   seen the salvation of our God.
Show yourselves joyful unto the Lord,
   all ye lands : sing, rejoice, and give
   thanks.

O come, let us sing unto the Lord : let
   us heartily rejoice in the strength of
   our salvation.
Let us come before his presence with
   thanksgiving : and show ourselves
   glad in him with Psalms.
For the Lord is a great God : and a
   great King above all gods.
In his hand are all the corners of the
   earth : and the strength of the hills is
   his also.
The sea is his, and he made it : and his
   hands prepared the dry land.
O come, let us worship, and fall down
   : and kneel before the Lord our
   Maker.
For he is the Lord our God : and we
   are the people of his pasture, and the
   sheep of his hand.
To day if ye will hear his voice, harden
   not your hearts : as in the
   provocation, and as in the day of

temptation in the wilderness;
When your fathers tempted me :
   proved me, and saw my works.
Forty years long was I grieved with
   this generation, and said : It is a
   people that do err in their hearts, for
   they have not known my ways.
Unto whom I sware in my wrath : that
   they should not enter into my rest.
Glory be to the Father, and to the Son
   : and to the Holy Ghost;
As it was in the beginning, is now,
   and ever shall be : world without
   end. Amen.
Psalm 95, Book of Common Prayer

O be joyful in the Lord, all ye lands :
   serve the Lord with gladness, and
   come before his presence with a
   song.
Be ye sure that the Lord he is God : it
   is he that hath made us, and not we
   ourselves ; we are his people, and
   the sheep of his pasture.
O go your way into his gates with
   thanksgiving, and into his courts
   with praise : be thankful unto him,
   and speak good of his Name.
For the Lord is gracious, his mercy is
   everlasting : and his truth endureth
   from generation to generation.
*Jubilate Deo, Psalm 100, Book of
Common Prayer*

Jesus and his prayer life

Jesus' parables about prayer

Most of the teaching Jesus gave on the subject came in the form of parables.

1. The parable of the friend at midnight

Here Jesus teaches that we need to be bold and persistent in praying: Luke 11:5-8.

2. The parable of the unjust judge

Here again the emphasis is on the boldness and persistence of the widow: Luke 18:1-8.

3. The parable of the Pharisee and the tax-collector

Here Jesus contrasts humility and penitence with a superior and proud attitude: Luke 18:10-14.

4. The parable of the unmerciful servant

Prayer needs to come from a loving and forgiving heart: Matthew 18:21-35.

Other teaching of Jesus about prayer

- Simplicity in prayer: see Matthew 6:5, 6; 23:14; Mark 12:38-40; Luke 20:47.
- Prayer should be taken seriously: see Mark 14:38.
- Christians should be united in their prayers: Matthew 18:19, 20.
- Prayer must be expectant: Mark 11:24.
- Prayer needs to be founded in faith: Mark 9:23.

Jesus' own prayer life

1. Jesus prayed on his own: see Luke 5:15, 16.
2. Jesus prayed through the night: see Luke 6:12.
3. Jesus prayed in times of spiritual conflict: John 12:20-28; Luke 22:39-46.
4. Jesus prayed with a grateful spirit: Luke 10:21; John 6:11; 11:41; Matthew 26:27.
5. Jesus prayed when he needed guidance: Luke 6:12-14.
6. Jesus prayed before his agony on the cross: Matthew 26:39.

Jesus' farewell prayer

The longest recorded prayer of Jesus that we have comes in John 17:1-26. It is sometimes called Jesus' high priestly prayer. It can be divided up as follows:

- Verses 1-5: Jesus prays for himself.
- Verses 6-19: Jesus prays for his disciples.
- Verses 20-26: Jesus prays for all believers.

Something to do

Read John 17:1-26 and give it your own title and see how you would split it up and name each section you split it into.

The Garden of Gethsemane

This garden, near the Mount of Olives, Matthew 26:30, was a favorite retreat of Jesus and his disciples. Jesus' intense prayer here, Luke 22:41, probably gave rise to Christians kneeling for prayer.

The prominence of prayer

Prayer in the Old Testament

The importance of prayer can be measured by the prominence given to it in the Scriptures and in the lives of those who have been used by God.

Even if one excludes the Psalms, there are numerous model prayers to be found in the Old Testament.

- Prayers of intercession: Genesis 18:16-33; Exodus 32:11-20.
- A prayer of confession: Ezra 9:5-15.
- A prayer of dedication: 2 Chronicles 6:14-42.
- A prayer of dependence: 2 Chronicles 20:6-12.
- A prayer for healing: Isaiah 38:3, 9-20.
- A prayer in a national crisis: 2 Kings 19:14-19.
- A prayer of thanksgiving: 1 Samuel 2:1-10.
- A prayer of recommitment: Jonah 2:2-9.
- A prayer for deliverance: Isaiah 37:14-20.
- A prayer for restoration: Daniel 9:4-19.

Something to do

Go through the above prayers and see what they teach about the person who is praying and about God the Father who answers prayer.

Paul's prayers

Paul encourages his readers that prayer should be like the trust that a tiny Hebrew child has in his dad when he holds out his hands to him in delight and says, *"Abba,"* that is, "Daddy." See Romans 8:15; Galatians 4:6.

Paul emphasized that prayer is a gift of the Holy Spirit, 1 Corinthians 14:14-16 and that believers pray "in the Spirit" Ephesians 6:18; Jude 20.

Paul constantly breaks out into prayer in the middle of his letters:

In Romans 1:8-12 he starts by pouring out his heart to God in gratitude.

In Ephesians 1:15-19 Paul gives thanks to God for all those who have come to know Jesus through his ministry.

In Ephesians 3:14-18 Paul prays that his fellow-Christians might know more of God's power in their lives.

In Colossians 1:9-11 Paul asks that his readers may know more about spiritual wisdom and understanding.

Something to do

Read through the above prayers and see what God teaches you about prayer through them.

Making use of written prayers

Jesus and hymn-singing

At every major Jewish festival the Hallel ("Praise") Psalms were sung. They were Psalms 113 to 118. Every Jewish boy learnt the Hallel Psalms by heart. At the end of the Lord's Supper, before Jesus and his disciples went to the Garden of Gethsemane, they sang the second part of the Hallel Psalms, psalms 115–118. "When they had sung a hymn, they went out to the Mount of Olives" Matthew 26:30.

Hymn-singing and revival have often gone hand in hand.

Using a hymn-book

Many of the great men of prayer have made use of a hymn-book in their own times of private prayer. A good Christian song-book or hymn-book need not be used only on Sundays.

If you are looking for Christian hymns on the Internet which you can listen to as well as read you could try the following site.

Web address: http://www.cartex.com/ hymnal/ **Title:** The Electronic Hymnal **Features include:** Audio music; musical score.

Short reflections and arrow prayers

"A good watchmaker is one who makes watches and prays: a good housemaid is one who sweeps and prays. Prayer may be equally with words or without: it may be 'Jesu, my God and my all.'" *E. B. Pusey*

Short prayers from the Bible

Speak, for your servant is listening.
Samuel, 1 Samuel 3:10, NRSV

Let the words of my mouth and the meditation of my heart be acceptable to you, O Lord, my rock and my redeemer. *Psalm 19:14, NRSV*

Wait for the Lord;
be strong, and let your heart
take courage;
wait for the Lord! *Psalm 27:14, NRSV*

O send out your light and your truth;
let them lead me;
let them bring me to your holy hill
and to your dwelling.
Psalm 43:3, NRSV

O God, you know my folly;
the wrongs I have done are not
hidden from you. *Psalm 69:5, NRSV*

Be pleased, O God, to deliver me.
O Lord, make haste to help me!
Psalm 70:1, NRSV

Will you not revive us again,
so that your people may rejoice
in you? *Psalm 85:6, NRSV*

Bless the Lord, O my soul,
and all that is within me,
bless his holy name.
Psalm 103:1, NRSV

Lord, save me! *Peter, Matthew 14:30*

Lord, help me. *A Canaanite woman, Matthew 15:25*

I believe, help my unbelief!
  Father of boy possessed by an unclean spirit, Mark 9:24

Here am I, the servant of the Lord; let it be with me according to your word. *Mary, Luke 1:38, NRSV*

God, be merciful to me, a sinner!
  Praying tax-collector, Luke 18:13

Jesus, remember me when you come into your kingdom.
  Penitent dying thief, Luke 23:42

My Lord and my God!
  Thomas, John 20:28

Come, Lord Jesus! *Revelation 22:20*

The grace of the Lord Jesus be with all the saints. Amen.
  Revelation 22:20, NRSV

Arrow prayers

Remember your mercies, Lord.

Be gracious to me, O God.

In you I hope all day long.

In your love remember me.

In you I place all my trust.

Awake, O my soul, awake!

God is worthy of our praise.

Create a clean heart in me.

Have mercy on me, O God.

Holy is the Lamb of God.

Jesus is the Lamb of God.
Glory to the Lamb of God.

Holy, holy, holy Lord.

My cup is overflowing.

Joy cometh in the morning.

I have been given mercy.

Taste and see that the Lord is good.

You are my strength and my song.

I will never forget you.

His eye is on the sparrow.

The Lord keeps the little ones.

How good is the Lord to all.

Fill me with joy and gladness.

Let the healing waters flow.

Oh, that we might know the Lord!

I have grasped you by the hand.

His love is everlasting.

I have called you by your name.

My peace is my gift to you.

Let go and let God.

Reverence for God

C. S. Lewis was in favor of using written prayers as well as extemporary ones. He wrote: "A few formal, ready-made, prayers serve me as a corrective of – well, let's call it 'cheek'."

Hannah More, 1745–1833, English educationalist and religious writer, wrote: "Written forms of prayer are not only useful and proper, but indispensably necessary to begin with."

Strengthen us, O God, to relieve the oppressed, to hear the groans of poor prisoners, to reform the abuses of all professions; that many be made not poor to make a few rich; for Jesus Christ's sake. *Oliver Cromwell*

O God, help us not to despise or oppose what we do not understand. *William Penn*

Change the world, O Lord, beginning with me. *A Chinese student*

Lord, give us faith that right makes might. Abraham Lincoln

The things, good Lord, that we pray for, give us the grace to labor for. *Thomas More*

O Lord God, when Thou givest to Thy servants to endeavor any great matter, grant us also to know that it is not the beginning, but the continuing of the same to the end, until it be thoroughly finished, which yieldeth the true glory; through Him who for the finishing of Thy work laid down his life, our Redeemer, Jesus Christ. *Source unknown, based on a saying of Sir Francis Drake*

Take from us, O God, all pride and vanity, all boasting and self-assertiveness, and give us the true courage that shows itself by gentleness; the true wisdom that shows itself by simplicity; and the true power that shows itself by modesty; through Jesus Christ our Lord. *Charles Kingsley*

Almighty God, the Protector of all who trust in you, without whose grace nothing is strong, nothing is holy, increase and multiply on us your mercy, that through your holy inspiration we may think the things that are right and by your power may carry them out, through Jesus Christ our Lord. *Martin Luther*

Teach me, my Lord Jesus, instruct me, that I may learn from you what I ought to teach about you. *William Laud*

O Lord, I am yours. Do what seems good in your sight, and give me complete resignation to your will. *David Livingstone*

Lord, make me an instrument of your peace.
Where there is hatred, let me sow love,
where there is injury, pardon,
where there is doubt, faith,
where there is despair, hope,
where there is darkness, light,
where there is sadness, joy.
O Divine Master, grant that we may not so much seek
to be consoled as to console,
not so much to be understood as to understand,
not so much to be loved as to love.
For it is in giving that we receive,
it is in pardoning that we are pardoned,
it is in dying that we are born to eternal life.
Attributed to Francis of Assisi

My dearest Lord,
be thou a bright flame before me,
be thou a guiding star above me,
be thou a smooth path beneath me,
be thou a kindly shepherd behind me,
today – tonight – and forever. *Columba*

We beg you, Lord, to help and defend us.
Deliver the oppressed,
have compassion on the despised,
raise the fallen,
reveal yourself to the needy,
heal the sick,
bring back those who have strayed from you,
feed the hungry,
lift up the weak,
remove the prisoners' chains.
May every nation come to know that you are God alone,
that Jesus is your Son,
that we are your people, the sheep of your pasture. *Clement of Rome*

O Lord, support us all the day long, until the shadows lengthen, and the evening comes, and the busy world is hushed, and the fever of life is over, and our work is done. Then, Lord, in your mercy grant us a safe lodging, and a holy rest, and peace at the last; through Jesus Christ our Lord. *Used by J. H. Newman. Based on a sixteenth-century prayer*

O Lord, forgive what I have been, sanctify what I am, and order what I shall be. *Author unknown*

Grant to us your servants: to our God – a heart of flame;
to our fellow men – a heart of love;
to ourselves – a heart of steel. *Augustine of Hippo*

Something to do

Try taking an arrow prayer, or short prayer, or even a much longer prayer into the day with you. Reflect on it during the day. See if you can remember it at the end of the day and think if you have learned any spiritual lesson from it.

Dearest Lord, teach me to be generous;
   teach me to serve you as you
deserve;
      to give and not to count the cost,
      to fight and not to heed the wounds,
      to toil and not to see for rest,
      to labor and not to seek reward,
      except to know that I do your will.
   Ignatius Loyola

Almighty God, in whom we live and move and have our being, you have made us for yourself and our hearts are restless until in you they find their rest. Grant us purity of heart and strength of purpose, that no selfish passion may hinder us from knowing your will, no weakness from doing it; but that in your light we may see light clearly, and in your service we may find our perfect freedom; through Jesus Christ our Lord. *Augustine of Hippo*

Grant me, I beseech thee, almighty and merciful God, fervently to desire, wisely to search out, truly to acknowledge, and perfectly to fulfill,

all that is well-pleasing to thee. Order thou my worldly condition to the honor and glory of thy name; and of all that thou requirest me to do, grant me the knowledge, the desire, and the ability, that I may so fulfill it as I ought, and as is expedient for the welfare of my soul. *Thomas Aquinas*

O Lord, thou knowest how busy I must be this day. If I forget thee, do not thou forget me. *General Lord Astley, before the battle of Edgehill*

Thanks be to you, my Lord Jesus Christ,
   for all the benefits you have won for me.
   For all the pains and insults you have borne for me.
   O most merciful Redeemer, Friend, and Brother,
      may I know you more clearly,
      love you more dearly,
      and follow you more nearly,
      day by day. *Richard of Chichester*

Father,
      give us wisdom to perceive you,
      intellect to understand you,
      diligence to seek you,
      patience to wait for you,
      eyes to behold you,
      a heart to meditate on you
      and a life to proclaim you,
      through the power of the Spirit
of our Lord Jesus Christ. *Benedict*

Lord Jesus Christ, you said that you are the Way, the Truth, and the Life.

Help us not to stray from you, for you are the Way;

nor to distrust you, for you are the Truth;

nor to rest on any other than you, as you are the Life.

You have taught us what to believe, what to do, what to hope, and where to take our rest.

Give us grace to follow you, the Way, to learn from you, the Truth, and live in you, the Life. *Desiderius Erasmus*

God be in my head,
   and in my understanding;
   God be in my eyes,
   and in my looking;
   God be in my mouth,
   and in my speaking;
   God be in my heart,
   and in my thinking;
   God be at my end,
   and at my departing.
Book of Hours, 1514

4 OVERCOMING PROBLEMS IN THE CHRISTIAN LIFE

CONTENTS

Introduction

If we are to persevere as Christians it is essential we know where to turn in the Bible for comfort, encouragement and direction. It's best not to wait until we are at our wits' end before studying the moment in Elijah's life when he felt like curling up and dying. By studying how godly people in the Bible faced problems we are better equipped to cope with similar problems today.

Christians are not meant to discount the help that may be given by psychiatrists, any more than they should refuse to go to doctors. But they should also recognize that each of us is a whole being, spirit as well as mind and body, and they should not ignore the spiritual malaise that is at the root of and is the cause of many physical and mental problems. It is therefore important to be fully conversant with the spiritual principles that are laid down in God's word.

If a correct remedy is to be applied, it is essential to diagnose a problem correctly. Paul had no doubt about the ultimate cause of all problems: "For our struggle is not against flesh and blood, but against the rulers, against the authorities, against the powers of this dark world and against the spiritual forces of evil in the heavenly realms" (Ephesians 6:12). These studies are designed to show how we may put on and use God's armor in this spiritual warfare.

Why do so many Christians collapse?

No easy answers

In the studies in this section the following procedure will be adopted.

1. The problem will be identified and analyzed.
2. The Bible's solution to the problem will be given.

We often find that it is not the Bible's teaching that we find hard to understand, but rather that it seems so hard to follow it in our own lives. In that sense there are no easy answers. The solution may be straightforward, but apparently impossible to put into practice.

But then who ever said that the Christian life would be a bed of roses? The one person who warned his would-be followers about the steep and rugged path ahead was Jesus. He said, "If anyone would come after me, he must deny himself and take up his cross and follow me" Matthew 16:24. And to "take up one's cross" meant the equivalent of being prepared to face the electric chair, just because one was a follower of Jesus.

Backsliding, apostasy

Perhaps one of the more neglected doctrines of scripture concerns backsliding, turning away from God, apostasy, falling away. It's not the kind of subject that preachers like to choose or congregations like to hear. But there is plenty of teaching on this subject in the Bible.

The problem
Jeremiah

Jeremiah, like a number of other Old Testament prophets, seems to have spent most of his ministry in calling people back to God, who had wandered away.

"'You have rejected me,' declares the Lord. 'You keep on backsliding.'" Jeremiah 15:6. The Israelites did not just turn their backs on God once, they made a habit of it. They kept on backsliding.

Paul

We usually think of backsliding in connection with some moral problem. However, the apostle Paul wrote his letter to the Galatians because they had embraced heretical teaching. Heresy and false teaching had made them backslide.

You can almost feel how upset Paul was about this situation when he wrote:

"Formerly, when you did not know God, you were slaves to those who by nature are not gods.

But now that you know God—or rather are known by God—how is it that you are turning back to those weak and miserable principles? Do you wish to be enslaved by them all over again?

You are observing special days and months and seasons and years! I fear for you, that somehow I have wasted my efforts on you." *Galatians 4:8-11*

The Galatians were starting to replace the gospel of grace with the teaching of the law.

Peter

Peter, in his second letter, writes to warn
Christians about false teachers who
"mouth empty, boastful words and, by
appealing to the lustful desires of sinful
human nature,...entice people who are
just escaping from those who live in
error" 2 Peter 2:18. Peter is making it
clear that these false teachers are
deliberately targeting new Christians by
attempting to seduce them back to their
old sinful ways.

Peter declares the dreadful logic of this
situation: "If they have escaped the
corruption of the world by knowing our
Lord and Savior Jesus Christ and are
again entangled in it and overcome, they
are worse off at the end than they were
at the beginning" 2 Peter 2:20.

The solution

The solution to this problem is as easy
to state as it is difficult to put into
practice. In a word it is to repent.

Jeremiah

Through the prophet Jeremiah, the Lord
says to his wandering people, "Return,
faithless people; I will cure you of
backsliding" Jeremiah 3:22.

If we go to a doctor with an ailment or
disease we have to tell him what it is
before he can prescribe a medicine or
cure. So returning to God involves
repenting and telling God about our
unfaithfulness, and turning away from
sin and back to him.

John

To the church at Ephesus, John puts it
in a nutshell when he writes, "Yet I hold
this against you: You have forsaken your
first love. Remember the height from
which you have fallen. Repent and do
the things you did at first" Revelation
2:4, 5.

Dealing with doubt

Pilgrim's Progress

John Bunyan's allegory about a Christian on his pilgrimage to heaven is the most biblical allegory that has ever been written. This extract homes in on the problem of doubt.

Now I saw in my dream, that they had not journeyed far, when the river and the way for a time parted, at which they were very sorry; yet they did not dare to go out of the way. Now the way from the river was rough, and their feet were very sore because of their travels; so the souls of the pilgrims were much discouraged because of the way. Numbers 21:4. So, as they went on, they wished for a better way. After a little there was on the left hand of the road a meadow, and a stile into it. That meadow is called By-path meadow. Then said Christian to his fellow pilgrim, If this meadow is on our way, let's go through it. Then he went to the stile and looked and saw that there was a path on the other side of the fence. This is just what I had hoped for, said Christian; here is a gentle path. Come, good Hopeful, let us go over the stile.

HOPEFUL: But what if this path leads us away from our route?

CHRISTIAN: That is unlikely, said the other. Look, see how it goes in the same direction as our route? So Hopeful, being persuaded by his fellow pilgrim, followed him over the stile. When they had gone over, and were going along the path, they found that it was very easy to walk along. Then they saw in front of them a man walking along, just as they were. His name was Vain-Confidence.

They called to him, and asked him where this path went.

He said, To the Celestial Gate.

Look, said Christian, did not I tell you so? We are on the right track. So they carried on walking behind Vain-Confidence. But when night came down, it became so dark that they lost sight of Vain-Confidence, who had been in front of them.

Then Vain-Confidence, who could not see what was in front of him, fell into a deep pit, which had been deliberately dug out by the owner of those grounds, to catch proud fools. He was killed by his fall. Isaiah 9:16.

Now, Christian and his fellow pilgrim heard him fall. So they called to him to see if he was hurt, but there was no answer. They just heard groaning. Then said Hopeful, Where are we now? Then his fellow pilgrim was silent, as he realized that he had led him out of the right way; and now it started to rain, with thunder, and lightning in a most terrible way.

Then Hopeful groaned in himself, saying, Oh that I had stuck to the other way!

CHRISTIAN: Who could have thought that this path should have led us out of the way?

HOPEFUL: I was afraid from the very beginning, and therefore warned you gently. I would have spoken more strongly, but you are older than I.

CHRISTIAN: Good brother, be not offended; I am sorry I have taken you from the way, and have put you in such imminent danger. Pray, my brother, forgive me; I did not do it from any evil motive.

HOPEFUL: Be comforted, my brother, for I forgive you; and believe, too, that this will be for our good.

CHRISTIAN: I am glad I have with me a merciful brother: but we must not stand here; let us try to go back again.

HOPEFUL: But, good brother, let me go first.

CHRISTIAN: No, if you please, let me go first, so if there is any danger, I may be first to find it, as I am to blame for leading us away from our path.

HOPEFUL: No, said Hopeful, you shall not go first, for as your mind is troubled it may lead you away from the way again. Then for their encouragement they heard the voice of one saying, "Take note of the highway, that road that you take." Jeremiah 31:21. But by this time the waters had greatly risen, which made going back very dangerous. (Then I thought that it is easier going out of the way when we are in, than going in when we are out.) Yet they

attempted to go back; but it was so dark, and the flood was so high, that as they tried to return they were nearly drowned nine or ten times. Neither could they, despite all their efforts, return to the stile that night. So, at last, they found a little shelter, where they sat down until dawn. But as they were so tired, they fell asleep. Now there was, not far from the place where they slept, a castle, called Doubting Castle, which was owned by Giant Despair. It was in his grounds they now were sleeping. So Giant Despair, after he had got up early in the morning, walked up and down in his fields, and discovered Christian and Hopeful asleep in his grounds. Then with a grim and surly voice, he told them to wake up. He asked them where they had come from and what were they doing in his grounds. They told Giant Despair that they were pilgrims, and that they had lost their way. Then said the giant, You have, last night, trespassed on me by lying on my grounds, and therefore you must go along with me. So they were forced to go, because he was stronger than they. They also had but little to say, for they knew themselves in a fault. The giant, therefore, drove them before him, and put them into his castle, into a very dark dungeon, nasty and stinking to the spirits of these two men. Here, then, they lay from Wednesday morning till

Saturday night, without one bit of bread, or drop of drink, or light, or anyone to ask how they might escape. In this evil trap they were far from friends and acquaintances. Psalm 88:18. Now in this place Christian had double sorrow, because it was through his foolish counsel that they were brought into this distress.

Now Giant Despair had a wife, and her name was Diffidence: so when he had gone to bed he told his wife what he had done, and that he had taken a couple of prisoners, and thrown them into his dungeon for trespassing on his grounds. Then he asked her also what he should do with them next. So she asked him who they were, where they came from, and where they were going, and he told her. Then she counseled him, that when he arose in the morning he should beat them without mercy. So when he arose, he took hold of a huge crab-tree cudgel, and went down into the dungeon to them. He beat them fearfully, in such a way that they were not able to help themselves. This done, he withdraws and leaves them there to condole their misery, and to mourn under their distress: so all that day they spent the time in doing nothing other than sighing with bitter lamentations.

The next night, Diffidence, talked again with her husband about them, and finding that they were still alive, advised him to tell them to commit suicide. So when morning came, he went to them in a gruff manner, as before, and perceiving them to be very sore with the stripes that he had given them the day before, he told them, that since they were never likely to come out of that place, the only thing they could do was to kill themselves, either with a knife, halter, or poison. For why, he said, should you choose to live, seeing that brings you so much bitterness? But they desired him to let them go. With that he became even more angry, and jumped on them and would have killed them himself, but he fell into one of his fits, and lost for a time the use of his hands. So he left them as before to consider what to do. Then did the prisoners consult between themselves whether it was best to take his counsel or no; and thus they began to talk.

CHRISTIAN: Brother, said Christian, what shall we do? The life that we now live is miserable. For my part, I do not know whether it is best to live, or to die. My soul wants to be strangled, and the grave is preferable to this dungeon. Job 7:15. Shall we be ruled by the giant?

HOPEFUL: Indeed our present condition is dreadful, and death would be far more welcome to me than to live here for ever. But let us consider, the Lord of the country to

which we are going has said, "Thou shalt do no murder," no, not to another man's person; much more, then, are we forbidden to take his counsel to kill ourselves. Besides, he who kills another, can but commit murder upon his body; but for one to kill himself, is to kill body and soul at once. And moreover, my brother, you talk of ease in the grave; but have you forgotten the hell to which murderers certainly go? For "no murderer hath eternal life," etc. And let us consider again, that all the law is not in the hand of Giant Despair: others, so far as I can understand, have been taken by him just as we have, and yet they have escaped out of his hands. Who knows but that God, who made the world, may cause that Giant Despair may die; or that, he may forget to lock us in; or that he may, in a short time, have another of his fits before

us, and may lose the use of his limbs? And if ever that should come to pass again, for my part, I am resolved to pluck up the heart of a man, and to try my utmost to get from under his hand. I was a fool that I did not try to do it before. But, however, my brother, let us be patient, and endure a while: the time may come when we are released. But let us not be our own murderers.

With these words Hopeful at present did moderate the mind of his brother; so they continued together in the dark that day, in their sad and doleful condition.

As evening approached, the giant went down into the dungeon again, to see if his prisoners had taken his counsel. But when he came there he found them alive; and truly, alive was all; for now, for lack of bread and water, and by reason of the wounds they received when he beat them, they could only just breathe. But I say, he found them alive; at which he fell into a grievous rage, and told them, that seeing they had disobeyed his counsel, it should be worse for them than if they had never been born.

At this they trembled greatly, and I think that Christian fell into a swoon; but coming a little to himself again, they renewed their discourse about the giant's counsel, and whether yet they had best take it or not.

That night Mrs Diffidence asked her husband Giant Despair if the two prisoners had taken his counsel. He replied, They are sturdy rogues; they choose rather to bear all hardships than to make away with themselves. Then said she, Take them into the castle-yard tomorrow, and show them the bones and skulls of those you have already killed and make them believe, that before the end of the week you will tear them in pieces, as you did to these fellows before them.

So when the morning came, the giant went to them again, and took them into the castle-yard, and showed them the bones and skulls as his wife had told him. These, he said, were once pilgrims, as you are, and they trespassed on my grounds, as you have done; and when I thought fit I tore them in pieces; and so within ten days I will do to you: get

down to your dungeon again. And with that he beat them all the way there. They lay, therefore, all day on Saturday in a lamentable state, as before.

Now, when night had come, and when Mrs Diffidence and her husband the giant were in bed, they started to speak to each other about their prisoners. The old giant was amazed that he could neither by his blows nor counsel kill them off. And with that his wife replied, I fear that they live in hopes that someone will come to rescue them; or that they have picklocks with them, and so they hope to escape. If that is the case, my dear, said the giant; I will search them in the morning.

Well, on Saturday, about midnight they began to pray, and continued in prayer till almost dawn.

Now, a little before it was day, good Christian, as one half amazed, brake out into this passionate speech: What a fool, he said, am I, to lie here in a stinking dungeon, when I may as well walk at liberty! I have a key on my person, called Promise, that will, I am persuaded, open any lock in Doubting Castle.

Then said Hopeful, That is good news; good brother, take out your key, and try it.

Then Christian pulled out his key and began to try it in the dungeon door, whose bolt, as he turned the key, gave back, and the door flew open with ease, and Christian and Hopeful both came out. Then he went to the outer door that leads into the castle-yard, and with his key opened that door also. Then he went to the iron gate, for that must be opened too; but that lock went desperately hard, yet the key did open it. They then thrust open the gate to make their escape with speed; but that gate, as it opened, made such a creaking, that it woke Giant Despair, who got up quickly to pursue his prisoners. But he felt his limbs fail him, for he had another fit, so that he could not go after them.

Then they went on, and came to the King's highway, and so were safe, because they were out of his jurisdiction.

Now, when they had gone over the stile, they began to consider what they should do at that stile, to prevent those who would come after them from falling into the hands of Giant Despair. So they agreed to erect a pillar, and to engrave on its side this sentence: "Over this stile is the way to Doubting Castle, which is kept by Giant Despair, who despises the King of the Celestial country, and seeks to destroy his holy pilgrims." Many, therefore, who followed after, read what was written, and escaped the danger. This done, they sang as follows:

"Out of the way we went,
and then we found
    What 'twas to tread upon
        forbidden ground:
    And let them that come after
        have a care,
    Lest heedlessness makes them
        as we to fare;
    Lest they, for trespassing, his
        prisoners are,
    Whose castle's Doubting, and
        whose name's Despair."
John Bunyan, Pilgrim's Progress

The devil

"The devil will do everything in his power to sow seeds of doubt in your mind as to whether your conversion is a reality or not." *Billy Graham*

Facing doubt with promise

Few Christians have never had doubts about whether they really are children of God. When faced with this doubt take the following action.

Confront your doubt with a promise from God's Word.

If you find the illustration in Revelation 3:20 particularly helpful go to it and tell yourself about the promise it contains. It says that Jesus "will come into" our lives when invited. If we did invite him into our lives, then no matter how many doubts we may have, we rely on God's promise. We no longer live in the grip of doubt.

The decline and fall of David

Recovering from blatant sin
Many Christians understandably react in the following way after they have committed some blatant and public sin. "I'm done for as a Christian. I'll keep clear of all my Christian friends. I won't go to church again, for I'm no hypocrite." And so after some terrible episode many Christians quietly fade away.

Look at David's life
If that should happen to us we should read about what happened to David.

He made such a promising start
He had killed the giant Goliath as he trusted in God's strength. He had defeated Israel's enemies. He had established Jerusalem as Israel's capital. He was ushering in a golden age for Israel.

Lesson No 1: Seasoned Christians and mature and godly people can and do fall into blatant sin.

Follow David as he declines
We don't look at David in 2 Samuel 11 in order to gloat over his mistakes. We only look at David in order to say, "There but for the grace of God go I."

- David shirked his responsibility and this led to idleness: 2 Samuel 11:1.
- David knew God's commands but decided to ignore them: 2 Samuel 12:9-10.
- Idleness can easily lead to

temptation. At any rate David was hardly "watching and praying" and so fell prey to temptation: 2 Samuel 11:2.
- Temptation led to sin. David desired another person's wife: 2 Samuel 11:3; Exodus 20:17.
- No matter how "big" or "little" we may consider a sin to be, it does not please the Lord: 2 Samuel 11:27.
- David commits adultery with Bathsheba: 2 Samuel 11:4; Exodus 20:14.
- David arranges for Bathsheba's husband, Uriah, to become drunk: 2 Samuel 11:12, 13; Habakkuk 2:15.

Lesson No 2: One sin leads to another sin.

- David plots Uriah's death: 2 Samuel 11:5-25; Exodus 20:13.

Lesson No 3: It is better to confess sin immediately instead of conniving to cover it up: Proverbs 28:13.

- David lived a lie and the life of a hypocrite, trying to cover up his sin.
- In this whole episode, everything that David did displeased the Lord: 2 Samuel 11:27.

Reflect on the sinfulness of sin
We have a tendency to read more about the victories and triumphs recorded in the Bible than about people's sins and shortcomings. But this part of David's life is recorded for us to learn from, just as we learn from his faithfulness to God.

From the story of David and Bathsheba, we learn that:

- if we don't master sin, it will master us;
- any sin committed deliberately is tantamount to not only despising God's commands, but to despising God himself: 2 Samuel 12:9, 10;
- we can be certain that our sin will find us out: 2 Samuel 12:1-9; Numbers 32:23;
- we should judge ourselves before thinking about condemning anyone else: 2 Samuel 12:5-7; Matthew 7:1-5;
- sin always has its consequences: 2 Samuel 12:8-12. Sin is contagious, in that it affects others;
- we reap what we sow: Galatians 6:7;
- through sin we can become a stumbling block to others: 2 Samuel 12:14;
- when we sin against another person we are sinning against God: Psalm 51:4;

- sin stains the heart: Psalm 51:2, 10;
- sin makes us deaf to God's still small voice: Psalm 51:8;
- sin makes us lose the joy of God's salvation: Psalm 51:12.

David's repentance

Alongside 2 Samuel 12:1-13, read Psalm 51:1-19. The heading written over the top of Psalm 51 in some Bibles reads: "A psalm of David. When the prophet Nathan came to him after David had committed adultery with Bathsheba."

- Humanly speaking David may have never recovered had it not been for the faithful and hard-hitting ministry of Nathan. Nathan rebukes David: 2 Samuel 12:1-4.
- Because of his hypocrisy, David is angry: 2 Samuel 12:5-6.
- David has his sin uncovered: 2 Samuel 12:7; Numbers 32:23.
- David begins to view sin as God views sin: 2 Samuel 12:8-12.
- David confesses his sin: 2 Samuel 12:13; Psalm 51:1-3.
- David asks to be cleansed: Psalm 51:7.

Lesson No 4: God's forgiveness is for sinners, not for the righteous: Matthew 9:13.

David's restoration

David served God faithfully for many years after his adultery. We remember David as a man after God's own heart, 1 Samuel 13:14.

Overcoming temptation

Will temptations ever cease?

Will there ever be a time when we grow out of temptation? The short answer is "No." It is a false hope to think that after being a Christian for ten years, or 20 years, one will no longer be tempted.

1. "I am like dry gunpowder"

This is how the Scottish minister, Robert McCheyne put it: "I am tempted to think that I am now an established Christian, – that I have overcome this or that evil desire so long, – that I have got into the habit of the opposite grace, – so that there is no fear; I may venture very near the temptation – nearer than other men. This is a lie of Satan. One might as well speak of gunpowder acquiring the characteristic of resisting fire, so that it

is not set alight by a spark. As long as powder is wet, it resists the spark; but when it becomes dry, it is ready to explode at the first touch. As long as the Spirit dwells in my heart, he deadens me to sin, so that I know that God will carry me through temptation. But when the Spirit leaves me, I am like dry gunpowder."

2. Jerome in the desert

Jerome cut himself off from the immediate temptations of city life. He went and lived in the desert. But, to his dismay, he still found that he was tempted. Here is part of a letter Jerome wrote to Eustochium about his wilderness experience.

"How often when I was living in the

desert, parched by a burning sun, did I fancy myself among the pleasures of Rome! Sackcloth disfigured my unshapely limbs, and my skin from long neglect had become as black as an Ethiopian's. And although in my fear of hell I had consigned myself to this prison, where I had no companions but scorpions and wild beasts, I often thought myself in the company of many girls. My face grew pale, and my frame chilled with fasting; yet my mind was burning with desire, and the fires of lust kept bubbling up before me when my flesh was as good as dead. Helpless, I cast myself at the feet of Jesus."

An additional fallacy about temptation
I must be a terrible sinner as I'm always being tempted

Actually, quite the opposite is true. We have to have it firmly lodged in our thinking that to be tempted is no sin at all. Giving in to temptation is where we go wrong. The classic scriptural example which demonstrates that temptation in itself is no sin is the temptations of Jesus in the desert, in Matthew 4:1-11. From this passage it is clear as crystal that Jesus himself was tempted by the devil. But Jesus never sinned. We conclude that being tempted is not a sin.

This is an important truth because some Christians collapse as soon as any temptation crosses their path. What should be remembered is that the devil only bothers to tempt growing Christians. He does not need to bother

with feeble, ineffective and unfaithful Christians. Robert McCheyne once observed: "I know well that when Christ is nearest, Satan is also busiest."

Coping with temptation

If we are right to conclude that temptations will attack us throughout our Christian lives, how are we to deal with it?

Veni, vidi, vici

A variation of Caesar's famous motto, "I came, I saw, I conquered," which he wrote in a letter after his victory at Zela, helps us to be on our guard against temptation. The variation to "I came, I saw, I conquered," is: "I saw, I desired, I took."

Eve

In Genesis 3:6, Eve *saw* the fruit, *desired* to eat the forbidden fruit, and then *took* it.

Achan

Achan's sin, recorded in Joshua 7:11: "When I *saw* in the plunder a beautiful robe from Babylonia, two hundred shekels of silver and a wedge of gold weighing fifty shekels, I *coveted* them and *took* them."

Three pieces of advice from Scripture

1. Make use of the Bible: Matthew 4:4, 7, 10; Psalm 119:11; 1 John 2:1.
2. Watch and pray: Matthew 26:41.
3. Rely on God's faithfulness which will give you an exit route: 1 Corinthians 10:13.

Getting the right guidance

A perplexing problem

Many Christians genuinely want to be
guided by God. They want to make the
correct decision about something in
their life. But the problem is: "Where do
I get the right guidance from? How does
God make his will known to me?"

My walk with Jesus

By far the most important factor in
knowing God's will is knowing God.
This means that the best way to find
God's guidance on a specific matter is to
be leading a healthy and faithful
Christian life.

The two key verses to have engraved
on our hearts when we seek guidance
are Proverbs 3:5, 6: "Trust in the Lord
with all your heart and lean not on your
own understanding; in all your ways
acknowledge him, and he will make
your paths straight."

What about my conscience?

If you are seeking God's guidance about
something that is specifically forbidden
in the Bible – forget it. Just don't do it.
God has already given all the guidance
you ever need.

But how much can we be influenced
by our consciences? If our conscience
tells us that something is okey, does that
mean that we can move ahead? And,
conversely, if our conscience tells us that
something is wrong, does that always
mean that we should not move ahead?

For a mature Christian who is well-versed in the teaching of the Bible the conscience can be a helpful guide. It is possible for us to play fast and loose with our consciences. One terrible result of totally overriding our consciences is mentioned in 1 Timothy 4:2: "Such teachings come through hypocritical liars, whose consciences have been seared as with a hot iron."

There is just one caveat here. We need to be taking steps to see that our consciences are being continually educated and informed by God's Word. All Christians should have clear consciences all of the time: 1 Peter 3:16.

Take some practical steps
None of the suggestions below are an infallible guide as you seek God's will on a specific matter in your own life, but they should help as you pray about and ponder which course to take.

1. Be guided by Christians friends
"A wise man listens to advice" Proverbs 12:15.

2. Use your mind
Don't spurn what has been called "sanctified common sense." Matthew 22:37 records Jesus saying that his followers should love God will all their "minds."

Some people find it a help to make two lists on a piece of paper. One list has all the factors that are in favor of a particular decision. The other list has all the factors that are not in favor of a specific course of action. Then you have to use your mind and make the decision.

A mini Bible study on guidance
Have this promise from the prophet Isaiah in the forefront of your mind: "The Lord will guide you always" Isaiah 58:11.

1. How does God guide us?

a. with his voice: John 10:27
b. with his eye: Psalm 32:8
c. with his counsel: Psalm 73:24
d. by his presence: John 10:4.

2. In which direction does God guide us?

a. along paths of peace: Luke 1:79
b. into all truth: John 16:13.

3. For how long will God guide us?

a. all the time: Isaiah 58:11
b. until we die: Psalm 48:14.

4. What conditions need to be fulfilled if I am to be guided?

a. Acknowledge God in all you do: Proverbs 3:5, 6.
b. Commit your way to the Lord: Psalm 37:5.

Psalm 73:24
One footnote concerning guidance. After you have been guided by God, don't forget to be grateful, as the psalmist was: "You guide me with your counsel" Psalm 73:24.

A word about holiness, worry and sickness

A word about holiness

One of the top priorities for a Christian should be to live a holy life.

God expects this of us. Paul wrote to a new Christian fellowship: It is "God's will that you should be holy" 1 Thessalonians 4:3.

Hebrews 12:10 reminds us that "without holiness no one will see the Lord."

The first Anglican bishop of Liverpool, J. C. Ryle, 1816–1900, wrote a book entitled "*Holiness*." In it he wrote:

I am convinced that the first step toward attaining a higher standard of holiness is to realize more fully the amazing sinfulness of sin.

Sound Protestant and Evangelical doctrine is useless if it is not accompanied by a holy life.

True holiness is much more than tears and sighs....A holy violence, a conflict, a warfare, a fight, a soldier's life, a wrestling are spoken of as characteristic of the true Christian.

True holiness does not consist merely of believing and feeling, but of doing and bearing, and a practical exhibition of active and passive grace. Our tongues, our tempers, our natural passions and inclinations – our conduct as parents and children, masters and servants, husbands and wives, rulers and subjects – our dress, our employment of time, our behavior in business, our demeanor in sickness and health, in riches and poverty – all, all these are matters which are fully treated by inspired writers.

I have had a deep conviction for many years that practical holiness and entire self-consecration to God are not sufficiently attended to by modern Christians in this country.

A word about worry

Jesus never taught that it did not matter if his followers were consumed by worry. So it's no good if we attempt to laugh off the fact that we worry so much by saying: "Yes, I do worry a lot. But then so do all Christians."

Jesus once said that to worry was to behave like a pagan! "So do not worry, saying, 'What shall we eat:' or 'What shall we drink?' or 'What shall we wear?' For *the pagans* run after all these things, and your heavenly Father knows that you need them" Matthew 6:31, 32.

A word about the antidote to worry

- God is the Christian pilgrim's companion through life: Genesis 28:15; Psalm 34:20.
- God watches over us like a sleepless watchman: Psalm 121:4.
- God as our almighty Guardian: 2 Timothy 1:12; 1 Peter 1:5; Jude 24: Revelation 3:10.
- God watches over our lives with infinite care: Psalm 115:12; Luke 12:7.
- "Cast all your anxiety on him because he cares for you" 1 Peter 5:7.

A word from John Newton about worry

I compare the troubles which we have to undergo in the course of the year to a great bundle of faggots, far too large for us to lift. But God does not require us to carry the whole at once. He mercifully unties the bundle, and gives us first one stick, which we are to carry today, and then another, which we are to carry tomorrow, and so on. This we might easily manage, if we would only take the burden appointed for each day; but we choose to increase our troubles by carrying yesterday's stick over again today, and adding tomorrow's burden to the load, before we are required to bear it.

A word about sickness

Are any among you sick? They should call for the elders of the church and have them pray over them, anointing them with oil in the name of the Lord. The prayer of faith will save the sick, and the Lord will raise them up. *James 5:14, 15*

Caring for the sick

Before all things and above all things, care must be taken of the sick, so that they may be served in very deed as Christ himself...But let the sick on their part consider that they are being served for God's honor, and not provoke their brethren who are serving them by their unreasonable demands. *Benedict, Rule*

Using sickness positively

Sickness helps to remind men of death.

Sickness helps to make men think seriously of God, and their souls, and the world to come.

Sickness helps to soften men's hearts, and teach them wisdom.

Sickness helps to level and humble us.

Sickness helps to try men's religion, of what sort it is.

The storms of winter often bring out the defects in a man's dwelling, and sickness often exposes the gracelessness of a man's soul. Surely anything that makes us find out the real character of our faith is a good. *J. C. Ryle*

A word about anger

A word about righteous anger

Not all anger is wrong. There is such a thing as righteous anger. Jesus demonstrated his righteous anger when he cleansed the temple.

"So he [Jesus] made a whip out of cords, and drove all from the temple area, both sheep and cattle; he scattered the coins of the money changers and overturned their tables. To those who sold doves he said, 'Get these out of here! How dare you turn my Father's house into a market!'" *John 2:15, 16.*

"Anybody can become angry – that is easy; but to be angry with the right person, and to the right degree, and at the right time, and for the right purpose, and in the right way – that is not within everybody's power and is not easy." *Aristotle*

"A person who does not know how to be angry does not know how to be good. And a person who does not know how to be shaken to his heart's core with indignation over evil things is either a fungus or a wicked person." *Henry Ward Beecher*

"Anger is one of the sinews of the soul. He who lacks it hath a maimed mind." *Thomas Fuller*

A word about the wrong sort of anger

A quick-tempered man does foolish things. *Proverbs 14:17*

A patient man has great understanding, but a quick-tempered man displays folly. *Proverbs 14:29*

A gentle answer turns away wrath, but a harsh word stirs up anger. *Proverbs 15:1*

Better a patient man than a warrior, a man who controls his temper than one who takes a city. *Proverbs 16:32*

A fool gives full vent to his anger, but a wise man keeps himself under control. *Proverbs 29:11*

My dear brothers, take note of this: Everyone should be quick to listen, slow to speak and slow to become angry, for man's anger does not bring about the righteous life that God desires. *James 1:19, 20*

"In your anger do not sin": do not let the sun go down while you are still angry. *Ephesians 4:26*

"Never answer an angry word with an angry word. It's always the second remark that starts the trouble." *Author unknown*

"To seek to extinguish anger utterly is but a bravery of the Stoics. We have better oracles: 'Be angry, but sin not.' 'Let not the sun go down upon your wrath.'" *Francis Bacon*

"A man is as big as the things that make him angry." *Winston Churchill*

"Anger is just one letter short of danger." *Author unknown*

"The wind of anger blows out the lamp of intelligence." *Author unknown*

"Never forget what a man says to you when he is angry." *Henry Ward Beecher*

"No matter how just your words may be, you ruin everything when you speak with anger." *John Chrysostom*

"The sun must not set upon anger, much less will I let the sun set upon the anger of God towards me." *John Donne*

"No form of vice, not worldliness, not greed of gold, not drunkenness itself, does more to un-Christianize society than evil temper. For embittering life, for breaking up communities, for destroying the most sacred relationships, for devastating homes, for withering up men and women, for taking the bloom off childhood; in short, for sheer gratuitous misery-producing power, this influence stands alone." *Henry Drummond*

"Beware the fury of a patient man." *John Dryden*

"There was never an angry man that thought his anger unjust." *Francis de Sales*

"Anger is never without a reason but seldom a good one." *Benjamin Franklin*

"Anger is the fever and frenzy of the soul." *Thomas Fuller*

"Anger is short-lived in a good man." *Thomas Fuller*

"You cannot acquire the gift of peace if by your anger you destroy the peace of the Lord." *Gregory the Great*

"He who angers you, conquers you." *Proverb*

"He that overcomes his anger conquers his greatest enemy." *Latin proverb*

"Be not angry that you cannot make others as you wish them to be, since you cannot make yourself as you wish to be." *Thomas à Kempis*

A word about persecution

A word about persecution

The arrogant mock me without restraint, but I do not turn from your law. *Psalm 119:51*

Bloodthirsty men hate a man of integrity and seek to kill the upright. *Proverbs 29:10*

He drew his bow and made me the target for his arrows. He pierced my heart with arrows from his quiver. I became the laughingstock of all my people; they mock me in song all day long. *Lamentations 3:12-14*

The words of Jesus

They persecuted me, they will persecute you. *John 15:20*

The experience of Paul

I consider that our present sufferings are not worth comparing with the glory that will be revealed in us. *Romans 8:18*

Up to this moment we have become the scum of the earth, the refuse of the world. *1 Corinthians 4:13*

Forty stripes save one. *2 Corinthians 11:24*

The teaching of Paul

In fact, everyone who wants to live a godly life in Christ Jesus will be persecuted. *2 Timothy 3:12*

The persecuted in the Old Testament remembered

Women received back their dead, raised to life again. Others were tortured and refused to be released, so that they might gain a better resurrection. Some faced jeers and flogging, while still others were chained and put in prison. They were stoned; they were sawed in two; they were put to death by the sword. They went about in sheepskins and goatskins, destitute, persecuted and mistreated–the world was not worthy of them. They wandered in deserts and mountains, and in caves and holes in the ground. *Hebrews 11:35-38*

Peter points to the example of Jesus

But how is it to your credit if you receive a beating for doing wrong and endure it? But if you suffer for doing good and you endure it, this is commendable before God. To this you were called, because Christ suffered for you, leaving you an example, that you should follow in his steps. *1 Peter 2:20, 21*

In our case [as Christians] we are hated for our name. *Athenagoras*

Jesus promised his disciples three things – that they would be completely fearless, absurdly happy and in constant trouble. *G. K. Chesterton*

Against the persecution of a tyrant the godly have no remedy but prayer. *John Calvin*

When your enemies see that you are so determined that neither sickness, fancies, poverty, life, death, nor sins discourage you, but that you will continue to seek the love of Jesus and nothing else, by continuing your prayer and other spiritual works, they will grow enraged and will not spare you the most cruel abuse. *Walter Hilton*

Christians have become the targets of opportunity to the thug regimes around the world, and they are many. What's going on now is monumental, and it's affecting millions, tens of millions, of people. We're talking not about discrimination, but persecution of the worst sort: slavery, starvation, murder, looting, burning, torture. *Michael Horowitz*

If the Devil were wise enough and would stand by in silence and let the gospel be preached, he would suffer less harm. For when there is no battle for the gospel it rusts and it finds no cause and no occasion to show its vigor and power. Therefore, nothing better can befall the gospel than that the world should fight it with force and cunning. *Martin Luther*

You can kill us, but you can't hurt us. *Justin Martyr*

One of the shocking untold stories of our time, is that more Christians have died this century [the twentieth century] simply for being Christians than in any century since Christ was born. *A. M. Rosenthal, The New York Times*

The servant of Christ must never be surprised if he has to drink of the same cup with his Lord. *J. C. Ryle*

Persecution for righteousness' sake is what every child of God must expect. *Charles Simeon*

The true Christian is like sandalwood, which imparts its fragrance to the axe which cuts it, without doing any harm in return. *Sundar Singh*

Persecution in the early church

Through zeal and envy, the most
faithful and righteous pillars of
the church have been persecuted even
to the most grievous deaths.
Clement of Rome

Let us therefore become imitators of
His endurance; and if we should suffer
for His name's sake, let us glorify Him.
For He gave this example to us in His
own person, and we believed this.
Polycarp

"Eighty and six years have I now
served Christ, and he has never done
me the least wrong; how, then, can I
blaspheme my King and my Savior?"
Polycarp, in reply to the Roman
Proconsul commanding him to swear
allegiance to Caesar, saying, "Swear,
and I will set thee at liberty; reproach
Christ." They are put to death, and
they gain new life. *Eusebius*

The church of Christ has been
founded by shedding its own blood,
not that of others; by enduring
outrage, not by inflicting it. *Jerome*

Persecutions have made the church
of Christ grow; martyrdoms have
crowned it. *Jerome*

[Nero] laid the guilt, and inflicted the
most cruel punishments, upon a set of
people who were held in abhorrence
for their crimes, and popularly called
Christians...Their sufferings at their
execution were aggravated by insult
and mockery, for some were disguised
in the skins of wild beasts and worried
to death by dogs, some were crucified,
and others were wrapped in pitched
shirts and set on fire when the day
closed, that they might serve as lights
to illuminate the night. Nero lent his
own gardens for these executions.
Tacitus

A word about depression

Read Psalms 42 and 43

Probably the best two psalms to read during a time of depression are Psalms 42 and 43. In them the psalmist asks himself the question: "Why are you downcast, O my soul." We usually say that talking to oneself is the first sign of madness. But the famous Welsh preacher, Dr Martyn Lloyd-Jones, used to say that one of the signs of spiritual life is to be like this psalmist and to ask questions of oneself. The second question the psalmist asked is similar to the first: "Why so disturbed within me?" Psalm 42:5. But in answer to these disturbing questions the psalmist replies: "Put your hope in God" Psalm 42:6.

William Cowper

The English poet, William Cowper, 1731–1800, wrote a number of well-known hymns, such as *O for a closer walk with God*, and *God moves in a mysterious way*. He was a close friend of John Newton and together they made a collection of hymns which became known as the *Olney Hymns*. Cowper suffered greatly from depression and Newton saved him from taking his own life on a number of occasions. Cowper wrote this poem about his depression.

I was a stricken deer

I was a stricken deer, that left the herd
Long since; with many an arrow deep
  infixt
My panting side was charg'd, when

I withdrew
To seek a tranquil death in distant
  shades.
There was I found by one who
  had himself
Been hurt by th'archers. In his side
  he bore,
And in his hands and feet, the cruel
  scars.
With gentle force soliciting the darts,
He drew them forth, and heal'd,
  and bade me live.
Since then, with few associates,
  in remote
And silent woods, I wander, far from
  those
My former partners of the peopled
  scene;
With few associates, and not wishing
  more.
William Cowper, 1731–1800,
(in his mental illness)

A word about perseverence

A word about perseverence

He will keep you strong to the end, so that you will be blameless on the day of our Lord Jesus Christ. *1 Corinthians 1:8*

We are hard pressed on every side, but not crushed; perplexed, but not in despair; persecuted, but not abandoned; struck down, but not destroyed. *2 Corinthians 4:8, 9*

You need to persevere so that when you have done the will of God, you will receive what he has promised. *Hebrews 10:36*

In the confrontation between the stream and the rock, the stream always wins – not through strength but through perseverance. *Author unknown*

Slow and steady wins the race. *Aesop*

Perseverence is the sister of patience, the daughter of constancy, the friend of peace, the cementer of friendships, the bond of harmony and the bulwark of holiness. *Bernard of Clairvaux*

If the biographer gives me credit for being a plodder, he will describe me justly. Anything beyond this will be too much. I can plod. I can persevere in any definite pursuit. To this I owe everything. *William Carey.*
Carey's reply, as an old man, to his nephew who asked if he might write his biography.

Permanence, perseverance and persistence in spite of all obstacles, discouragements, and impossibilities: It is this, that in all things distinguishes the strong soul from the weak. *Thomas Carlyle*

There must be a beginning to any great matter, but the continuing to the end until it be thoroughly finished yields the true glory. *Francis Drake*

The value of good work depends on perseverance. You live a good life in vain if you do not continue it until you die. *St Gregory*

Only a sweet and virtuous soul, Like seasoned timber, never gives. *George Herbert*

Few things are impossible to diligence and skill. Great works are performed, not by strength, but perseverance. *Samuel Johnson*

Be of good cheer. Do not think of today's failures, but of the success that may come tomorrow. You have set yourselves a difficult task, but you will succeed if you persevere; and you will find joy in overcoming obstacles. Remember, no effort that we make to attain something beautiful is ever lost. *Helen Keller*

The drop of rain maketh a hole in the stone, not by violence, but by oft falling. *Hugh Latimer*

All things are possible to him who believes,
   yet more to him who hopes,
   more still to him who loves,
   and most of all to him who practices and perseveres in these three virtues. *Brother Lawrence*

Perseverance is a great element of success. If you only knock long enough and loud enough at the gate, you are sure to wake up somebody. *Henry Wadsworth Longfellow*

Victory belongs to the most persevering. *Napoleon*

If I have ever made any valuable discoveries, it has been owing more to patient attention, than to any other talent. *Isaac Newton*

Let me tell you the secret that has led me to my goal. My strength lies solely in my tenacity. *Louis Pasteur*

Nothing of great value in life comes easily. *Norman Vincent Peale*

There are only two creatures that can surmount the pyramids, the eagle and the snail. *Eastern proverb*

You're looking at a man who spent two years trying to learn to wiggle his big toe. *Franklin Roosevelt, when asked how he could do so much without being tired, referring to his recovery after polio*

By perseverance the snail reached the ark. *C. H. Spurgeon*

Our motto must continue to be perseverance. And ultimately I trust the Almighty will crown our efforts with success. *William Wilberforce, message to the Anti-Slavery Society, during his 45-year battle to outlaw the slave trade*

A word about trials

A soldier's prayer

I asked God for strength, that I might achieve,
I was made weak, that I might learn humbly to obey.
I asked for health, that I might do greater things,
I was given infirmity, that I might do better things.
I asked for riches, that I might be happy,
I was given poverty, that I might be wise.
I asked for power, that I might have the praise of men,
I was given weakness, that I might feel the need of God.
I asked for all things, that I might enjoy life,
I was given life, that I might enjoy all things.
I got nothing that I asked for –
but everything that I had hoped for,
almost despite myself, my unspoken prayers were answered.
I am among all men most richly blessed.

A Soldier's Prayer, written by an anonymous confederate soldier, in the US civil war

A pastor's poem

I ask'd the Lord, that I might grow
In faith, and love, and ev'ry grace,
Might more of his salvation know,
And seek more earnestly his face.
'Twas he who taught me thus to pray,
And he, I trust has answer'd pray'r;
But it has been in such a way,
As almost drove me to despair.
I hop'd that in some favor'd hour,
At once he'd answer my request:
And by his love's constraining pow'r,
Subdue my sins, and give me rest.
Instead of this. he made me feel
The hidden evils of my heart;
And let the angry pow'rs of hell
Assault my soul in ev'ry part.
Yea more, with his own hand he seem'd
Intent to aggravate my woe;
Cross'd all the fair designs I schem'd,
Blasted my gourds, and laid me low.
Lord, why is this, I trembling cry'd,
Wilt thou pursue thy worm to death?
"'Tis in this way," the Lord reply'd,
I answer pray'r for grace and faith.
These inward trials I employ,
From self and pride to set thee free;
And break thy schemes of earthly joy,
That thou mayst seek thy all in me.

John Newton

A word about pride

Warnings against pride
The Bible is full of warnings against pride.

> When pride comes, then comes disgrace, but with humility comes wisdom. *Proverbs 11:2*

> Pride goeth before destruction, and an haughty spirit before a fall. *Proverbs 16:18, KJV*

> Seest thou a man wise in his own conceit? There is more hope of a fool than of him. *Proverbs 26:12, KJV*

> Do not be proud, but be willing to associate with people of low position. *Romans 12:16*

> Let him that thinketh he standeth take heed lest he fall. *1 Corinthians 10:12, KJV*

Yet more warnings against pride
More verses to heed concerning pride are:

- Psalm 10:2; 73:6; 119:21
- Proverbs 6:17; 13:10
- Hosea 7:10
- Habakkuk 2:4
- 1 John 2:16.

Examples of proud people in the Bible
1. Pharaoh: Exodus 5:2
2. Naaman: 2 Kings 5:11
3. Uzziah: 2 Chronicles 26:16
4. Hezekiah: 2 Chronicles 32:25
5. Haman: Esther 3:5
6. Nebuchadnezzar: Daniel 4:30
7. Belshazzar: Daniel 5:23

Examples of spiritual pride
As you look up the following Bible references note how they are all examples of people who considered themselves to be very religious, or were members of a Christian fellowship.

1. The Pharisee in Jesus' parable about the Pharisee and the tax-collector: Luke 18:11
2. In some Pharisees: John 9:41
3. The arrogance of some Corinthian Christians: 1 Corinthians 4:18
4. Some members of the church of Laodicea: Revelation 3:17

What pride can lead to
1. Conceit
   a. In the Old Testament see Proverbs 3:7; 26:5; Isaiah 5:12.
   b. In the New Testament see Romans 12:16b; 1 Corinthians 8:2.
2. Haughtiness
   a. In the Old Testament see 2 Samuel 22:28; Isaiah 3:16; 16:6; 24:4; Jeremiah 48:29; Zephaniah 3:11.
3. Boasting
   a. In the Old Testament see Psalm 49:6; Proverbs 20:4; 25:14; 27:1; Daniel 3:15.
   b. In the New Testament see James 3:5; 4:16.

Pride is the only disease known to man that makes everyone sick except the one who has it. *Author unknown*

Remember that pride leads to hell, but humility to heaven! God always beats down the proud, and lifts up the humble. *Isaac Ambrose*

The demons are aware that the devil fell from heaven through pride, so they attack first those who are advanced in the way, by trying to set them against each other through pride. In this way they attempt to cut us off from God. *Antony of Egypt*

Other sins find their vent in the accomplishment of evil deeds, whereas pride lies in wait for good deeds, to destroy them. *Augustine of Hippo*

Those who wish to be praised in themselves are proud.
Augustine of Hippo

One of our most heinous and palpable sins is pride. This is a sin that has too much interest in the best of us, but which is more hateful and inexcusable in us than in other people.
Richard Baxter

The greatest fault is to be conscious of none. *Thomas Carlyle*

They that know God will be humble; they that know themselves cannot be proud. *John Flavel*

A cold, self-righteous prig who goes regularly to church may be far nearer to hell than a prostitute. *C. S. Lewis*

According to Christian teachers, the essential vice, the utmost evil, is pride. Unchastity, anger, greed, drunkenness, and all that, are mere fleabites in comparison: it was through pride that the devil became the devil: pride leads to every other vice: it is the complete anti-God state of mind. *C. S. Lewis*

God sends no one away empty except those who are full of themselves.
Dwight L. Moody

Pride, or the loss of humility, is the root of every sin and evil.
Andrew Murray

I pray God to keep me from being proud. *Samuel Pepys*

Be not proud of race, face, place, or grace. *Samuel Rutherford*

Learn to break your own will. Be zealous against yourself! Allow no pride to dwell in you.
Thomas à Kempis

Dealing with pride

Pride is like a beard. It just keeps growing. The solution? Shave it every day. *Author unknown*

When you become like a child, your pride will melt away and you will be like Christ himself in the stable at Bethlehem. *Martin Luther*

Our pride must have winter weather to rot it. *Samuel Rutherford*

The source of pride

Pride comes from a deeply buried root – it comes from the devil himself. Where pride is fostered a person will be insincere, harsh, bitter, cutting, disdainful. *F. Fénelon*

Why pride matters

The source of sin is pride. *Augustine of Hippo*

Pride made the soul desert God, to whom it should cling as the source of life, and to imagine itself instead as the source of its own life. *Augustine of Hippo*

Without a doubt it is pride that is the greatest of sins. *Bernard of Clairvaux*

Pride causes us to use our gifts as though they came from ourselves, not benefits received from God, and to usurp our benefactor's glory. *Bernard of Clairvaux*

The more proud anyone is himself, the more impatient he become at the slightest instance of it in other people. And the less humility anyone has, the more he demands and is delighted with it in other people. *William Law*

You can have no greater sign of a confirmed pride than when you think you are humble enough. *William Law*

Mini Bible study on pride

1. Pride is:
    a. a sin: Proverbs 21:4
    b. hated in God's sight: Proverbs 16:5
    c. forbidden: 1 Samuel 2:3
    d. the cause of being unclean: Mark 7:20, 22
    e. hardening the mind: Daniel 5:20.
2. Pride is characteristic of:
    a. the devil: 1 Timothy 3:6
    b. the world: 1 John 2:16
    c. false teachers: 1 Timothy 6:3, 4
    d. the wicked: Romans 1:30.
3. Pride leads people to:
    a. have contempt for and reject God's Word: Jeremiah 43:2
    b. self-deception: Jeremiah 49:16.

A word about stewardship

Principles of stewardship

There are many principles about Christian stewardship taught in the Bible. Sometimes the New Testament is less specific than the Old Testament about how much money we should give to God's work. In general terms the Old Testament says that this should be 10% of our income; the New Testament gives no percentage, but it does give principles.

1. Give freely

"Freely you have received, freely give" Matthew 10:8. This reference is to do with healing the sick, raising the dead, cleansing lepers, and driving out demons. Stewardship is a very broad term and should never be limited to money and how much we put in the collection plate on Sundays. It is concerned with us using to the full the great gifts God has given to each of us.

2. Giving brings blessing

"In everything I did, I showed you that by this kind of hard work we must help the weak, remembering the words the Lord Jesus himself said: 'It is more blessed to give than to receive.'" Acts 20:35. This is the only saying of Jesus we have that does not come in the four Gospels. As Paul was saying goodbye to the elders at Ephesus, whom he knew he would never see again, the last recorded words of his which he left ringing in their ears, was this previously unrecorded saying of Jesus: "It is more blessed to give than to receive." Paul wanted to drive home the point that if they followed this principle of giving, then God would indeed bless them.

3. Be a good steward

"Each one should use whatever gift he has received to serve others, faithfully administering God's grace in its various forms" 1 Peter 4:10. The spirit which says how should I use "my" time, "my" talents, "my" money is quite absent here. Everything we have is ultimately a gift from the hand of God. So nothing we have is really ours. We don't "own" real estate. At best, any land, buildings, or possessions we may have are "lent" to us. We hold them in trust. They are for the benefit of others, not for us just to feather our own nest with.

11 New Testament proverbs about stewardship

1. Where your treasure is there your heart will also be. See Matthew 6:21.
2. Don't cast your pearls before swine. See Matthew 7:6. This proverb applies to those who are called to Christian teaching. Here they are reminded they should always teach according to the spiritual capacity of their audience.
3. Give freely, as you have freely received. See Matthew 10:8. See also the first point in the above section.
4. Give to the state what belongs to the state and give to God what belongs to God. See Matthew 22:21.
5. If you have been entrusted with a lot, a great deal will be expected from you. See Luke 12:48.
6. Anybody who can be trusted with a little will be trusted with much more. See Luke 16:10-12. The principle here is that faithfulness is not determined by how much we are entrusted with but by our characters. Whatever we have been given, we have to be faithful in the way we use it.
7. It is more blessed to give than to receive. See Acts 20:35. See also the second point in the above section.
8. If you don't provide for your own family you are behaving like somebody who is even worse than an unbeliever. See 1 Timothy 5:8.
9. When we die we take nothing with us. See 1 Timothy 6:7.
10. The love of money is the root cause of so much evil. See 1 Timothy 6:10. This verse is often misquoted as: "Money is the root of all evil." That is not what this verse is saying. The problem is not money, but our "love" of money.
11. It's impossible for a person of faith not to do good deeds. See James 2:14-17. While it remains true that it is only genuine faith in Jesus that brings us salvation, it is also true that genuine faith will also produce good deeds.

Wearing God's armor

Problems, problems, problems

Many of the pages of this chapter have homed in on our problems. Many of the problems we face are the same problems that non-Christians face, even if we may deal with them differently. However, some of the problems Christians face, do not trouble non-Christians at all. But no matter what problems we face, Christians go into the battle in God's strength.

How to engage in the spiritual war

Ephesians 6:10-18 is Paul's final piece of teaching for the beloved Christians at Ephesus. He wants them to be strong in the Lord, so he tells them to equip themselves spiritually.

1. Identify the enemy

It's probably true that most Christians hardly give a passing thought to the devil. In Ephesians 6:11 Paul had mentioned "the devil's schemes." Now, in Ephesians 6:12 Paul reminds us of the reality and power of our enemy. "For our struggle is not against flesh and blood, but:

- against the rulers,
- against the authorities,
- against the powers of this dark world and
- against the spiritual forces of evil in the heavenly realms."

It is because we are, or at least should be, all too conscious of the devil that we:

- put on God's armor: Ephesians 6:11
- do not give the devil a foothold: Ephesians 4:27
- are alert to the devil, that lion who is always prowling around, looking for some unsuspecting Christian he can gobble up for supper: see 1 Peter 5:8
- resist the devil: James 4:7.

2. Put on the armor

As you "put it on" in your mind, note that it is all defensive armor. There is no defensive armor for the back, as we are not meant to be on the run from the enemy. So, a Christian who is ready for the battle wears:

- *the belt of truth* buckled round his

waist: Ephesians 6:14. Honesty also binds Christians together for the battle: Ephesians 4:15, 25.

- *the breastplate of righteousness*: Ephesians 6:14. Purity and being right with God are the characteristics of God's soldiers. See Ephesians 5:3.
- *feet fitted with the readiness that comes from the gospel of peace*: Ephesians 6:15. The gospel of peace brings harmony to the Christian fellowship. See Ephesians 4:3.
- *the shield of faith*: Ephesians 6:16. The Christian's confidence and hope are placed in God who will shield us from the flaming arrows of the evil one, just as the Roman shield, covered in leather and soaked in water, put out the flame-tipped arrows of the enemy. See Ephesians 3:20.
- *the helmet of salvation*: Ephesians 6:17. The more we identify with Jesus' followers and remember that we are members of his body, the more assured we become of our salvation. See Ephesians 3:6.

3. Use your weapon

- *the sword of the Spirit*, which is the word of God: Ephesians 6:17.

4. The Christian's secret weapon

- *pray in the Spirit*: Ephesians 6:18.

In all our spiritual battles we depend on God's strength, his word, and on God himself, through prayer.

Spiritual battles

In the spiritual battles which Christians face each day, we need to stand:

- in the faith: 1 Corinthians 16:13;
- in God's grace: Romans 5:2;
- in the gospel: 1 Corinthians 15:1;
- in our Christian freedom: Galatians 5:1;
- in the Lord, and in his mighty power: Philippians 4:1;
- not relying on any human wisdom: 1 Corinthians 2:5.

5   *SHARING MY CHRISTIAN FAITH*

CONTENTS	
	page

Introduction

Christians are not all called to be evangelists, but they are all called to be witnesses to Christ. This chapter has many studies on witnessing, but starts with personal evangelism. Every Christian should know what to do when asked: "How do I become a Christian?" The first chapter of John's Gospel tells of Andrew bringing his brother Peter to Jesus. "Andrew, Simon Peter's brother, was one of the two who heard what John had said and who had followed Jesus. The first thing Andrew did was to find his brother Simon and tell him, 'We have found the Messiah' (that is, the Christ). And he brought him to Jesus" (John 1:40-42). Commenting on this, Archbishop William Temple wrote, "This is the greatest service that one person can do another."

We are adept at making excuses for not engaging in personal evangelism: That's the minister's job; I'm just not that way inclined; I wouldn't be any good at it anyway; I don't know how to go about it.

The studies in this chapter could be described as a do-it-for-yourself manual on personal evangelism. But this might convey the wrong impression. For they emphasize the biblical teaching on how we should lead someone to trust Christ, and emphasize that salvation is not a conjuring trick we play on people as soon as we have a bit of know-how, but is God's work.

Are you motivated for personal evangelism?

The problem

Let's face it square on. Most Christians do not engage in any form of personal evangelism at all. This would all change if we all had the right kind of motivation.

What should our motivation be?

A good way to approach this topic is to see what motivated Jesus, who is our example in all things, 1 Peter 2:21, and then apply those things to ourselves. This will ensure that we are motivated in the right way.

Jesus was motivated by his compassion for the lost

We may often recall that Jesus had compassion on the crowds because of their physical hunger: see Matthew

15:32. We may often recall that Jesus had compassion on individuals because of their sickness: see Matthew 14:14. But we may not recall so often that Jesus was moved to the depths of his being when he was confronted by the spiritual needs of people. "When he [Jesus] saw the crowds he had compassion on them, because they were harassed and helpless, like sheep without a shepherd" Matthew 9:36.

Jesus asked for prayer

In response to seeing a crowd of spiritually needy people Jesus did two things. First of all he asked his disciples to pray. "The harvest is plentiful but the workers are few. Ask the Lord of the harvest, therefore, to send out workers into his harvest field" Matthew 9:37-38.

Jesus took action

After prayer Jesus did something himself about the situation. He selected and then sent out his disciples: Matthew 10:1, 5-7.

Two questions

If we've never managed to take the plunge and engage in any type of personal witness for Jesus there are a couple of questions we could be asking ourselves.

> • **Question 1:** Have I ever felt deep love and compassion for those who don't know Jesus?
>
> • **Question 2:** Shouldn't I be doing something about all the lost souls I meet?

If we frankly have little inclination to be involved in this sort of thing and if we don't feel too bothered about those who don't know Jesus we need to let God teach us to love.

As John put it, "We love because he [God] first loved us" 1 John 4:19. The more we meditate on God's love for us, John 3:16, especially as this love is seen focused in Jesus' death on the cross, the more we will love non-Christians.

Jesus had a clearly defined aim

Jesus told his disciples that his work was to carry out the work his Father had given him, and that he had to complete this work: see John 4:34. Jesus often spoke about doing his Father's will and pleasing his Father: John 5:30, 36; 6:38; 17:4; 19:28-30.

How do we stay motivated?

The best way to do this is to meditate on God's Word. This, for example, is about Jeremiah.

Stage 1: Excuses

To start with he was full of excuses when God called him to be his spokesman: Jeremiah 1:6.

Stage 2: "Eating" God's Word

Things changed for Jeremiah as he meditated and read and studied and "ate" God's Word. "When your words came, I ate them; they were my joy and my heart's delight, for I bear your name, O Lord God Almighty" Jeremiah 15:16.

Stage 3: Proclaiming God's Word

Jeremiah had a really rough time. As he spoke up for God he was ridiculed, reproached and mocked: see Jeremiah 20:8. Nevertheless Jeremiah persevered and could even write: "But if I say, 'I will not mention him or speak any more in his name,' his word is in my heart like a fire, a fire shut up in my bones. I am weary of holding it in; indeed, I cannot" Jeremiah 20:9.

No short-cuts

There are no short-cuts to being rightly motivated for personal evangelism. We just have to think how motivated Jesus was, and to meditate on God's Word, until, with Paul, we cry out: "Woe to me if I do not preach the gospel!" 1 Corinthians 9:16.

How do we get started on personal evangelism?

Orders and power

We've been given our marching orders: "Go and make disciples of all nations" (Matthew 28:19)

We know that the source of power for this does not rest in ourselves, but comes from God. Hence Paul could say: "I am not ashamed of the gospel, because it is the power of God for the salvation of everyone who believes" Romans 1:16.

But just where do we start? Do we have to pick a far-off country and go and evangelize there? Well, God certainly does call some to do that. But for most of us it means being a witness for Jesus just where we are.

The Institute For American Church Growth

If you were to ask the Institute For American Church Growth what the most effective way to reach people for Jesus is today, they could give you lots of statistics from a questionnaire of theirs which asked 10,000 people this question: "What was responsible for your coming to Christ and this church?"

This is how they analyzed the answers:

- I had a special need – 3%
- I just walked in – 3%
- I liked the minister – 6%
- I visited there – 1%
- I liked the Bible classes – 5%
- I attended a gospel meeting – 0.5%
- I liked the programs – 3%
- A friend or relative invited me – 79%.

Friendship evangelism

One possible conclusion to draw from this poll is that the most effective form of evangelism is friendship evangelism. Each of us has a circle of family and friends whom we know like nobody in the world knows. In that sense we are in a unique position.

101 ways

There are countless ways in which we can pass on the Good News about Jesus:

- by a personal invitation to church;
- by giving a Christian book;
- by giving away a Christian tract;
- by suggesting some Christian Internet sites;
- by telling a person how you became a friend and follower of Jesus;
- by praying for someone to become a Christian;
- by praying for an evangelist or minister;
- by supporting missionary work at home or abroad;
- by joining a team on a Christian holiday;
- by explaining how to become a Christian;
- by being friendly and neighborly;
- by writing a letter in which you explain how to become a Christian;
- by lending a CD or video.
- "I have become all things to all men so that by all possible means I might save some" 1 Corinthians 9:22.

Will you be rejected?

Once we're rightly motivated to start witnessing, once we have at least one person on our prayer list whom we regularly pray will become a Christian, once we've done all that, why do we still hesitate? Probably the number one reason for not starting any kind of one to one evangelism is our fear of being rejected.

We're out to please God not curry favor with people

When the first disciples started to preach the gospel they were met with mixed reactions. Some of them were thrown into prison for their trouble. When they were released on the condition that they never preached about Jesus again, Peter and John replied courageously, "Judge for yourselves whether it is right in God's sight to obey you rather than God. For we cannot help speaking about what we have seen and heard" Acts 5:19, 20.

Boldness

Have you ever thought about praying that God would make you bold in this?

Or have you ever thought of asking another Christian to pray that you will be strengthened by God so you can witness?

The mighty apostle Paul felt his need of asking for just this. At the end of his letter to the Ephesians, he writes: "Pray also for me, that whenever I open my mouth, words may be given me so that I will *fearlessly* make known the mystery of the gospel" Ephesians 6:19. And in the following verse he says the same thing. "Pray that I may declare it [the gospel] *fearlessly*, as I should" Ephesians 6:20.

"What must I do to follow Jesus?"

Answering the question

Here is a very straightforward way to help someone who asks you this question.

There are many different ways of answering this question and what follows is just one suggestion. Take from it what you find helpful and make it your own. You may care to adapt it greatly or just leave it as it is.

A. B. C.

This acrostic is really meant to be more for your benefit, than for the benefit of the person you are talking with. It's just a simple way of remembering how you are going to present the gospel is a very simple way.

Many people who have never tried to explain how a person can become a follower of Jesus before want to know exactly what to say.

A stands for admit

Some people think that they are followers of Jesus if they:

- keep the Ten Commandments
- do good deeds
- lead a good life
- go to church
- Never commit sexual sins
- donate money to charities.

If you can picture yourself now with a person who is asking the question: "What must I do to follow Jesus?" it **is** important that you make it clear that your answer to this question is not your own idea on the subject but that your answer is the answer found in the Bible.

You know that the Bible teaches that "our righteous acts are like filthy rags" Isaiah 64:6. The only thing we contribute to our salvation is our sin. Titus 3:4, 5 puts this truth clearly: "But when the kindness and love of God our Savior appeared, he saved us, not because of righteous things we had done, but because of his mercy."

Nobody can earn a place in heaven. It is God's gift: see Romans 6:23; Ephesians 2:8, 9. All this is vital for you to understand. But in order to keep the A.B.C. answer to the question "What must I do to follow Jesus?" short and simple, it suggests that you restrict yourself to just sharing one verse from the Bible under each of the four headings.

The first verse to share, which explains "A stands for something to admit" is Romans 3:23. Say to the person you are with:

> To answer the question: "What must I do to follow Jesus?" the first step to take involves admitting to God that, far from being perfect, we are, in his eyes, sinful. We could call this first step, step A. And A stands for admit. We need to admit that we are sinners. Here is a helpful verse in the Bible which explains this: (Then read from your Bible Romans 3:23, "for all have sinned and fall short of the glory of God.")

Then say something like:

> The first step we have to take is to be willing to own up to God that we are sinful in his sight, and that we want to have our sin to be forgiven by him.

This step is easy enough to understand with one's mind. It is quite logical to say that we are imperfect and that God is perfect. However, the idea that we are sinful in God's sight, needs to be admitted to by the person you are with. To agree with this is only possible if God's Spirit is at work in the person's life.

If the person you are with, let's call him/her, John/Mary, is happy to take this first step move on to the second step. You could say:

> "That's the first step to take, John/Mary. Okey? There are three steps to take. Now we move on to the second step."

B stands for believe

Humankind's problem is that we are sinful. God's solution to this was to send Jesus into our world so that he could die for our sins. When we were still sinners Jesus died for us: 1 Corinthians 15:3, 4; Romans 5:8; 2 Corinthians 5:21. These are the verses you need to bear in mind as you explain this second step.

Say:

> The second step, step B stands for "believe." The next verse I'm going

to turn explains this. (The verse for you to look up in your Bible is Isaiah 53:6.) It's a verse where the prophet Isaiah pictures us all being like sheep who have strayed: "We all, like sheep, have gone astray, each of us has turned to his own way; and the Lord has laid on him the iniquity of us all."

You could then say:

> This verse says that everyone in the world has gone astray and turned their backs on God. We have all gone our own way, and have rejected God's way. This is the meaning of what the Bible calls "sin." But then, the verse goes on to say that God has taken our sin and put it on Jesus.

Then explain this same truth by using your two hands. You will need some object to place on your hand that is big enough to cover it, such as a big book. (As this object is going to represent sin it may be best not to use your Bible.)

Now say something like this to John/Mary.

> This is a way that I have found helpful to understand what this verse says. It is a picture of what Jesus was doing when he died on the cross. My right hand is me, and my left hand is Jesus (at this point hold out your hands with the palms facing upwards). My right hand stands for me and for every other person in the

world. Isaiah is saying that we are weighed down with sin. So this book (which you now place on top of your right hand) is a picture of sin which drags me down all the time. When Jesus died on the cross he took my sin (now transfer the book from your right hand to your left hand) on him. This is what it means when we say that Jesus died for my sins. My sins were placed on him. So you see how I am now (move your right hand up and down a little)? My sin has been taken away and forgiven. It rests (move your left hand with the book still on it up and down a little) on Jesus. Jesus paid the penalty for my sins when he died on the cross. (Now put the book down and stop holding out your hands.)

Continue speaking and say:

So the second step to take to become a friend of Jesus involves believing something about Jesus. Step B stands for believe. I have to believe that Jesus died for me and for my sin when he died on the cross. That's steps A and B. Okey so far? The last step is step C.

C stands for committing myself to Jesus

The verses you need to bear in mind at this stage are Acts 16:3, John 3:16 and John 6:47, which say that anyone who believes in Jesus will be saved.

Say:

C stands for commit. We have to commit ourselves to Jesus. We have to respond to Jesus. It's time for us to do something. We commit ourselves to Jesus by handing over our lives to him, by asking him to run our lives. One picture the Bible uses to explain this is in the next verse I'm going to read. (Read Revelation 3:20.) Jesus is speaking and he says, "Here I am! I stand at the door and knock. If anyone hears my voice and opens the door, I will come in and eat with him, and he with me."

At this point it is very useful to have a postcard, which are sold in Christian bookshops, of Revelation 3:16. It is a painting of this verse by Holman Hunt, showing Jesus standing outside a door and knocking on it. If you have this picture you can explain what follows by pointing to different parts of the picture. You can now introduce the picture by saying:

I have a picture here which depicts this verse.

Continue by saying:

This verse pictures the Lord Jesus standing outside the door of someone's life. He is knocking on the door asking, as it were, if he can come in. This is how we start to be followers of Jesus. We ask him into our lives. This is what it means to commit ourselves to Jesus. We tell Jesus that we really do want him in our lives. Is this what you John/Mary would like?

If the person you are with says "yes," you could immediately pray a prayer of commitment to Jesus. However, to ensure that you are not pushing John/Mary into doing something he/she is not ready for, you may think it wise to offer the following alternative. If John/Mary say he/she does not want to take this step of commitment now, you could also suggest this alternative.

" John/Mary, if you would like to commit yourself to Jesus now I have a prayer that you could pray. But if you would prefer not to do this right now, you could pray the prayer on your own when you are ready to. So what would you like to do, John/Mary, take this step now, or take it later?"

If the person you are with indicates that he/she would like to commit their lives to Jesus right now you could say:

"That's great John/Mary. The way to commit yourself to Jesus is to invite him into your life. I have a short prayer here, which I could pray out aloud, line by line, and which you could pray after me, line by line, in your heart. Or if you prefer, you can pray it line by line out aloud:

"Dear Lord Jesus, (pause)
I admit that I am a sinner and need
    your forgiveness, (pause)
I believe that you died for me, (pause)
and my sin on the cross, (pause)
I now commit myself to you, (pause)
please come into my life. (pause)
Amen."

D stands for details

Now that John/Mary has asked the Lord Jesus Christ into his/her life there are five things for you to do. There's no need to mention to John/Mary that D stands for details (!) this is just for your benefit.

1. Instruct John/Mary of the necessity of Baptism.
2. Encourage John/Mary that Jesus really has come into his/her life.
3. Give John/Mary some introductory Bible Reading notes.
4. Ensure that John/Mary is linked up with a church
5. Pray

1. Assurance

Say:

John/Mary, this is so wonderful, that you have just asked the Lord Jesus into your life. If you ever have doubts about this in the future look up this last verse we read, Revelation 3:20, and read the last bit. There Jesus says, "I will come in." This is Jesus' promise to you. This is what he has done. So if you ever have doubts about this, you can recall that your faith does not rest on how strong you feel, but on Jesus' promise which he never breaks.

2. Reading the Bible

Give some introductory notes to John/Mary, explaining that they suggest short Bible passages which can be read every day, along with a few helpful words of explanation.Be brief. Don't give a sermon about the Bible.

3. Linking up with a church

Make sure that John/Mary is linked up with a helpful church. If John/Mary is not already linked up it's up to you to ensure that this happens.

4. Pray

Perhaps your greatest responsibility concerning John/Mary is that you should pray for him/her, especially over the next seven days.

Practical tips

If you follow the above outline there are a number of things that may help you:

Write out an outline

If you are new to all this and if you think that you may be a bag of nerves and forget everything that you should say, do this. At the back of your Bible write down as follows:

a. A for admit: Romans 3:23
b. B for belief: Isaiah 53:6
c. C for commit: Revelation 3:20.

If you forget what comes next you at least have this outline, and the three crucial Bible verses noted down to jog your memory.

Have a copy of Holman Hunt's picture with you

Have a copy of the prayer of

commitment with you

This you can then give to John/Mary if they want to go away and think things over. So when they do want to commit themselves to Jesus, they have this prayer to help them.

Have a set of Bible Reading notes

These need to be introductory ones, which just give readings and comments for a week or two. This booklet, as well as the Holman Hunt postcard will be available at your local Christian bookshop.

Have a pencil and paper/notebook

You need to be very sensitive about taking somebody's name and address and phone number, and about giving out details about yourself, in case someone misconstrues your intention. But if you think it's okey and you need the person's address (in order to link him/her up with a church, for example) ensure that you are not searching for a biro at this stage.

Watch your breath

Have a mint in your pocket so that any bad breath is not a problem.

A little homework

To help you to go over, in a little more depth, the basic Bible teaching about the Christian faith, here are a few verses to look up and ponder over.

- Verses about our guilt: Romans 1:18–3:20; especially 1:21-24, 28; 2:1-6, 21-24; 3:9; Ephesians 2:1-3; Galatians 6:7, 8; 1 Timothy 6:3-10.
- Verses about our helplessness: Isaiah 59:1, 2; Proverbs 28:13; Luke 13:1-5.
- Verses about Jesus being the Savior: Matthew 1:20, 21; John 1:29; 3:14-21 (compare with Numbers 21:4-9); John 5:22-24; 14:6; Acts 4:8-12; 1 Corinthians 15:1-11; 1 John 1:5-9; 5:9-13.
- Verses about receiving Jesus: John 3:14-16; 5:24; Romans 4:18–5:2; 10:8-10; 1 John 2:22-25; 3:21-24; 4:15; 5:11-13.

Personal evangelism and the New Testament letters

All of the New Testament letters

The New Testament letters teach both about personal evangelism and about the responsibilities all Christians have concerning non-Christians. These studies will pick one passage from each New Testament letter, except for 2 John and 3 John, as well as from the book of Revelation on these topics. From them we will see that the early church treated this subject with the utmost seriousness and were always encouraging each other to serve Jesus in this way.

Romans

Read Romans 1:14-16.

What has been called the three great "I am"s about personal evangelism are found here.

1. I am bound: Romans 1:14

Paul said he was bound to both Greeks and to non-Greeks. Paul lived his life as if he was under a great obligation. It was as if he felt that he had no choice but to pass on the gospel message.

2. I am eager: Romans 1:15

In fact Paul says, "I am so eager" to preach the gospel in Rome. God had given Paul an insatiable appetite to preach the gospel.

3. I am not ashamed: Romans 1:16

Far from being ashamed to be a witness for Jesus, Paul longed to travel to Rome so that he could preach in the capital city of the Roman world.

1 Corinthians

Read 1 Corinthians 9:22.

Paul became all things to all men so that some people would be saved. He says that to the weak he became weak, in order to win the weak to Jesus. For example, Paul himself had no qualms about eating meat that had been sacrificed to idols. But he knew that some Christians were not happy about this. So in order not to offend them Paul did not exercise the freedom he had in this matter. Paul's principle here was to help people find salvation, even if this meant he had to forego what he regarded as a legitimate practice.

2 Corinthians

Read 2 Corinthians 5:20.

Paul thought of himself, and all other Christians, as God's ambassadors.

We are Jesus' personal representatives. When Jesus died on the cross he represented us. Now we are told that we have to represent Jesus to those who are not Christians. Just as ambassadors represent their governments in a foreign country, so Christians today are in the world as Jesus' ambassadors.

In this verse Paul also says that he implored his readers to be reconciled to Christ. That is a good definition of the work Christian ambassadors should be engaged in.

Galatians

Read Galatians 1:23.

Paul never forgot that he had once

persecuted Christians. But he did not allow his non-Christian past to stop him from preaching about faith in Jesus. In fact it encouraged him to redouble his efforts in being an evangelist and teacher of the Christian faith. No matter what our past has been we can be Jesus' witnesses today.

Ephesians

Read Ephesians 6:19, 20.

Paul asked other Christians to pray for him in his work of preaching the gospel. Some Christians today neglect to ask fellow-Christians to pray for them and for their witness for Jesus. The one thing Paul asked prayer for was that he should be "bold" in his preaching of the gospel.

Paul's preaching landed him in prison. But he did not languish in prison, feeling sorry for himself. Rather he described himself as an "ambassador in chains." He continued to represent Jesus wherever he was.

Philippians

Read Philippians 2:15.

Paul urges his Christian friends at Philippi to stand out from the crowd. In a crooked and depraved world they are to be different. There should be a great contrast between them and the unbelieving world. They were to shine like stars. See Matthew 5:15, 16.

Colossians

Read Colossians 4:5, 6.

Paul tells his readers to think carefully about their Christian witness. He told them to be wise in the way in which they related to others. In this verse he also told them to make the most of every God-given opportunity. They were to maximize every opportunity for witness, not just allow them to slip by.

Sometimes, the impression people gain from Christians is that they are exceedingly argumentative and devoid of all human graces. In verse 6 Paul says that we should have only a pinch of salt in our witnessing, but that we should be full of grace. Also we should "know" how to answer everyone. If we find that we are stumped by an argument put forward by a non-Christian, it is up to us not to rest until we have found out what the answer is.

1 Thessalonians

Read 1 Thessalonica 2:4.

Paul reminds the young Christians at Thessalonica that it is a great privilege to witness for Jesus. They are to remember that God approves of personal witness and that they have been entrusted by God with the gospel. There is no greater work to engage in than helping to spread the gospel.

And, adds Paul, we are to do this in a way that pleases God, even if that should upset people. For God knows our hearts.

2 Thessalonians

Read 2 Thessalonians 3:2.

Some Christians feel that any kind of witness for Jesus is totally beyond them. Here Paul sets out one way to help to spread the gospel, even if we can never leave our homes. We are to pray. The specific prayer Paul asks for is that the Christians at Thessalonica should pray that he will be delivered from evil people who were quite prepared to physically attack Christian preachers.

1 Timothy

Read 1 Timothy 2:3.

Paul tells timid Timothy to remember that it is God's wish that people are saved. So when Timothy engaged in evangelistic work he should recall that he is doing what God himself approves of.

2 Timothy

Read 2 Timothy 2:10.

Paul tells Timothy that no suffering is too great if it is found while he is actively witnessing to Jesus. In this verse Paul also gives an excellent definition of what the aim of all Christian witnessing is.

It should be so that people "obtain the salvation which is in Christ Jesus." And not only that but that this salvation comes with "eternal glory," which is the final state of salvation. To be engaged in personal evangelism is to be working for people's salvation.

Titus

Read Titus 3:9-11.

Have you ever thought about the amount of energy, time and money that some Christians put into arguing against other Christians over matters of secondary importance. These verses warn the Christian worker not to get dragged into such fruitless activities. They should not spend all their time arguing about "foolish controversies." Or rather, they should not even join in such arguments and quarrels.

Philemon

Read Philemon verse 10.

Paul never restricted evangelism to working for people to cross over from the kingdom of darkness into the kingdom of light. No. Paul was always concerned that new, weak Christians should grow and become mature in Jesus.

Somehow, the runaway slave, Onesimus, had found Paul in prison in Rome. And through Paul he had become a Christian. As far as Paul was concerned it would have suited him if Onesimus had stayed in Rome and helped Paul. But Paul wanted what was best for Onesimus. Paul knew that if Onesimus returned to Philemon he was in danger of death. For the Roman law said that a master could kill a runaway slave. So Paul wrote this letter to his Christian friend Philemon, telling him to have Onesimus back. Some Christians are called to help repair relationships.

This may seem to be a far cry from personal evangelism. But it is not. It often flows from it.

Hebrews

Read Hebrews 5:12.

Here the writer to the Hebrews hands out a stinging rebuke to some of his readers. These people were not recent converts. By this time they should have been mature Christians. But instead of eating meat they still lived and thought like babies, drinking milk. Christian workers are not meant to neglect their own souls. They should feed on spiritual food so that they are spiritually strong themselves. They should not forever remain like children at school. They should be teachers.

James

Read James 5:18.

This verse is full of irony. In it James is ticking off anyone who thinks that faith and deeds can exist independently of each other. For a Christian every action should be the result of faith. It's never right to separate faith and deeds. It's not a question of: either, or. It's always: both, and.

1 Peter

Read 1 Peter 3:15, 16.

These verses should be learned by heart. They are so important in personal evangelism. They give such helpful guidelines about how to effectively speak for Jesus.

1. In your hearts

First of all, says Peter, never forget your own walk with Jesus. It's no good engaging in door-to-door witnessing seven nights a week if you don't have Jesus as Lord in your own heart.

2. Be prepared

If we are asked why we are Christians we should be able to give a good answer. We are able to do this because we have thought about it and we have prepared an answer to this question.

3. How to give an answer

Two characteristics should always be present in speaking to others about Jesus. We should have genuine respect for the person we are speaking to, and everything that we say should be said with gentleness. Now gentleness is hardly a characteristic of our age. But it should be the mark of a Christian.

2 Peter

Read 2 Peter 1:9 and 2 Peter 5-8.

All witnessing Christians long to be effective and fruitful. These verses tell us how to avoid being ineffective and unfruitful. For, presumably, in Peter's day, as in our own day, there are plenty of Christians around who lead ineffective and unfruitful lives.

So what is the secret? First of all be prepared for some hard work. In verse 5 Peter says, "make every effort." Idle, couch potato Christians are not in view here.

And what type of hard work are we meant to do? Peter gives a very full answer in these verses.

- We are not to be content with just having faith: we must add goodness to our faith.
- We are not to be content with just having faith and goodness: we must add knowledge to our goodness and faith.
- We are not to be content with just having faith, goodness and

knowledge: we must add self-control to our knowledge, goodness and faith.

- We are not to be content with just having faith, goodness, knowledge and self-control: we must add perseverence to our self-control, knowledge, goodness and faith.
- We are not to be content with just having faith, goodness, knowledge, self-control and perseverence: we must add godliness to our perseverence, self-control, knowledge, goodness and faith.
- We are not to be content with just having faith, goodness, knowledge, self-control, perseverence and godliness: we must add brotherly kindness to our godliness, perseverence, self-control, knowledge, goodness and faith.
- We are not to be content with just having faith, goodness, knowledge, self-control, perseverence, godliness and brotherly kindness: we must add love to our brotherly kindness, godliness, perseverence, self-control, knowledge, goodness and faith.

These are the virtues that will produce a fruitful Christian life.

1 John
Read 1 John 4:14, 15.

Here John uses two verbs which should be a spur to everyone involved in Christian witness. John says his readers are to "testify," and to "acknowledge." In each case they are to bear witness to Jesus. Christian witness may sometimes sink into self-centeredness. John says that our witness should always focus on Jesus: Jesus the Savior of the world, and Jesus the Son of God.

Jude
Read Jude 22, 23.

How should we witness to those who have doubt? We should be merciful towards them.

How should we witness to those who are on the verge of spiritual destruction? We should act in a most pro-active way. We should snatch them out of the fire. Jude reminds his readers that they should have more than one string to their bows. Their Christian witness should be appropriate and tailor-made for each individual they witness to.

Revelation
Read Revelation 2:10.

John warns the church in Smyrna about the persecution they are about to go through. He does not say that they should run away from it. He tells them:

- not to be afraid
- to remember that the devil is behind all persecution of Christians
- that some Christians well be imprisoned
- that some Christians will be martyred, but
- that these Christians will receive the crown of life.

Characteristics of a soul-winner

Romans 1:1-16 records some of the characteristics all soul-winners need.

- Soul-winners need to be set apart for the gospel: Romans 1:1.
- Soul-winners need to be prayerful all the time: Romans 1:9.
- Soul-winners need to long to be involved in evangelism: Romans 1:10.
- Soul-winners need to expect a spiritual harvest: Romans 1:13.
- Soul-winners need to have a passion for souls: Romans 1:15.
- Soul-winners need to be bold: Romans 1:16.
- Soul-winners need to have salvation as their message: Romans 1:16.

What does a witness for Jesus need to be ready for?

- A witness for Jesus needs to be ready to preach the gospel: Romans 1:15.
- A witness for Jesus needs to be ready to give an answer for his/her Christian hope: 1 Peter 3:15.
- A witness for Jesus needs to be ready to do good deeds: Titus 3:1.
- A witness for Jesus needs to be ready to be generous and share: 1 Timothy 6:18.
- A witness for Jesus needs to be ready to suffer for Jesus: Acts 21:13.
- A witness for Jesus needs to be ready to die for Jesus: 2 Timothy 4:6.
- A witness for Jesus needs to be ready to meet the Lord: Luke 12:40; 2 Timothy 4:6, 8; 1 John 2:28.

Learning from Jesus

John's Gospel

John records more of the conversations Jesus had with people than any other Gospel writer. One of the best ways to learn about personal evangelism is to read from the Gospels about all the different people who talked with Jesus. There are certain things to look for in these conversations.

1. Did Jesus ask a question?
2. If Jesus did ask a question, why did he ask that particular one?
3. Was there any difference in the person after he/she had been speaking with Jesus? If there was a difference what was it?

Jesus the soul-winner

John 4:4-34 shows Jesus, the soul-winner, at work. Just read through this story and see what you can learn about soul-winning.

You need to be in a place where you will find non-Christians: John 4:4. Some Christians are so caught up with Christian activities that they rarely meet non-Christians.

You need to know how to start a conversation: John 4:7; Matthew 5:47.

You need to remember that non-Christians are often very ignorant about spiritual matters: John 4:10; 1 Corinthians 2:14.

You must get to the point in the conversation that you can speak about spiritual things in general and God's gift in particular: John 4:10; Romans 6:23.

You must draw spiritual lessons from ordinary things: John 4:10-12. Think of all the ordinary things Jesus spoke about in his parables: harvests, fishing, a lost sheep, a judge, etc.

What you say must be spiritually satisfying: John 4:13, 14; Psalm 107:9.

At some point you must bring the person you are talking with face to face with their sin: John 4:16; Numbers 32:23.

Don't allow yourself to be side-tracked: John 4:19-21.

Don't let the moment go if you think that the person should be challenged about making a decision for Jesus: John 4:25; 2 Corinthians 6:2.

Trust God to reveal Christ through his Word. So use your Bible, or quote from the Bible: John 4:26; Matthew 16:16, 17.

Encourage new Christians to become involved in serving Jesus: John 4:35, 36; 39.

Paul's witness to Jesus

1. Paul's attitude

Paul was an egghead. Had he lived in America today he would have walked off with the top honors at Harvard. Had he lived in England today he would have his M.A. hood from Oxford or Cambridge hanging on the back of his study door. He had studied under the very best professor of theology of his day: Gamaliel. See Acts 5:34 and 22:3.

Paul dedicated his great brain to the work of founding churches and building them up and caring for them.

However, Paul did not rely on his brain, he relied on God, and the grace of God he had discovered in the Lord Jesus Christ.

- Paul trusted in God's grace: 2 Corinthians 12:9.
- Paul boasted about his personal weakness so that Jesus' power might rest on him: 2 Corinthians 12:9.
- Paul could even delight in difficulties and being persecuted: 2 Corinthians 12:10.
- Even when Paul was hard pressed, he was not crushed: 2 Corinthians 4:8.
- Even when Paul was perplexed, he did not despair: 2 Corinthians 4:8.
- Even when Paul was persecuted, he knew that Jesus had not abandoned him: 2 Corinthians 4:9.
- Even when Paul was struck down, he knew that he was not destroyed: 2 Corinthians 4:10.
- Paul knew that all his present suffering could not be compared to his future glory: Romans 8:18.

2. Paul's aims

Paul's aims as a Christian can be summed up by saying that Paul was focused on Jesus Christ. He did this:

- by counting himself dead to his sinful desires: Romans 6:11;
- by being alive to God in Christ Jesus: Romans 6:11;
- by bearing the marks of Jesus on his body: Galatians 6:17;
- by preaching only about Jesus and Jesus' death: 1 Corinthians 2:2;
- by boasting only in the cross of Jesus: Galatians 6:14.

3. Paul's suffering

Paul does not hide the fact that he suffered a great deal for Jesus. When he was still called Saul, before his conversion experience on the Damascus Road, Paul knew what it was to mete out persecution to Christians, as he rounded them up for imprisonment. But now the tables were turned. Paul had to endure suffering as a follower of Jesus.

Paul never brags about his suffering, although he not infrequently refers to this in his letters so that other Christians may learn a lesson from his suffering, or may be encouraged in their own witness for Jesus.

- Paul was frequently put in prison: 2 Corinthians 11:23.
- Paul was frequently severely flogged: 2 Corinthians 11:23.
- Paul was frequently exposed to death: 2 Corinthians 11:23.
- Paul received at least 149 lashes from the Jews: 2 Corinthians 11:24.
- Paul was beaten three times with rods: 2 Corinthians 11:25.
- On one occasion Paul was stoned and left for dead: 2 Corinthians 11:25.
- On his evangelistic travels Paul was ship-wrecked three times: 2 Corinthians 11:25.
- Once Paul spent a whole night and day adrift in the sea: 2 Corinthians 11:25. "I spent a day and a night in the open sea."

- Paul was constantly on the move, often hounded out of the city by men seeking his death: 2 Corinthians 11:26.
- Paul was in danger from rivers: 2 Corinthians 11:26.
- Paul was in danger from bandits: 2 Corinthians 11:26.
- Paul was in danger from his fellow countrymen: 2 Corinthians 11:26.
- Paul was in danger from Gentiles: 2 Corinthians 11:26.
- Paul was in danger at sea: 2 Corinthians 11:26.
- Paul was in danger from false Christians: 2 Corinthians 11:26.
- Paul often worked so hard that he went without sleep: 2 Corinthians 11:27.
- Paul knew what it was to be hungry and thirsty and to have no food: 2 Corinthians 11:27.
- Paul knew what it was to be naked and cold: 2 Corinthians 11:27.
- On top of everything else Paul had to bear the pressure of his concern for all the churches: 2 Corinthians 11:27.
- Paul was prepared to be a fool for Jesus' sake: 1 Corinthians 4:11.
- Paul was sometimes reduced to going around in rags: 1 Corinthians 4:11.
- Paul was sometimes homeless: 1 Corinthians 4:11.
- Paul was often slandered: 1 Corinthians 4:13.

He/she who wins souls is wise

Soul-winning

"Soul-winning," or "winning souls" are not phrases that all Christians like to use. The objection to these phrases is that they may make people think that Jesus is not concerned about the whole person, but just about his soul. Now we know that this is not true. For Jesus healed people physically when he was on this earth. What the phrase "soul-winning" is trying to emphasize is that people do have souls. For people need more than education, food, and entertainment. "Winning souls" is a phrase that is underlining the need that everybody has: and that this need includes a great spiritual need.

Proverbs 11:30

Proverbs 11:30 says, "He who wins souls is wise." This is one of the best mottos in the Bible for soul-winners.

Key things for soul-winners to remember
The Holy Spirit alone makes soul-winning possible

The first disciples had to wait in Jerusalem until the Holy Spirit came on them in power. Only then could they carry out Jesus' command to be witnesses. None of our witnessing is any good at all unless it is done in the name of Jesus and in the power of the Holy Spirit. See Acts 1:8.

Be motivated by love of God

Our motivation should not just be that we are carrying out orders. Our motivation should that we are compelled to do this because of Jesus' love: 2 Corinthians 5:14.

Don't witness in your own strength

Jesus said to his followers that he would make them fishers of men. We seek to join the ranks of those who have been faithful witnesses to Jesus in every century and rely on Jesus in our witnessing. See Matthew 4:19.

Seek God's guidance about what you should say

a. Moses was told that God would teach him what to say: Exodus 4:12.
b. Isaiah knew what it was to have God's words put in his mouth: Isaiah 51:16.
c. Paul wrote about words that did not come from conventional human wisdom but of words taught by the Spirit: 1 Corinthians 2:13.

There's nothing wrong with having high ambitions about soul-winning

Paul made no bones about the fact that he was out to win as many people as possible for Jesus even if it meant great sacrifice: see 1 Corinthians 9:19.

We must continually seek wisdom from Jesus in this work

See Matthew 13:36.

We must be alert to all the tricks of the devil in this work

See Matthew 13:38, 39.

Where are we to win souls?

The short answer to this question is: wherever we are. We should seek to win souls:

At home

The demon-possessed man, whom Jesus healed, was specifically told by Jesus to witness to him in his home. "Go home to your family and tell them how much the Lord has done for you" Mark 5:19.

Witnessing at home is often the most difficult place for some Christians to witness, and is sometimes the last place they think of when it comes to soul-winning.

Peter must have been eternally grateful that his brother Andrew introduced him to Jesus: see John 1:40-42.

Among friends

What Andrew did for his brother Peter, Philip did for Nathanael. Philip told Nathanael to come with him to meet Jesus. As a result of this Nathanael become one of Jesus' twelve disciples. See John 1:45-49.

Among neighbors

The first thing the woman from Samaria did after she had met up with Jesus was to tell her neighbors about him. See John 4:28-30. We may sometimes think that people should not be encouraged to witness about Jesus for quite some time after they became Christians, or not before they have gone through some training course. There is great wisdom in

being trained to be an effective witness for Jesus. But in the example of this Samaritan woman there are two remarkable things to note.

a. She told her neighbors about Jesus, even though she clearly did not fully understand if he was even the Christ. See John 4:29.
b. Her witnessing to Jesus was greatly blessed by God. "Many of the Samaritans from that town believed in him [Jesus] because of the woman's testimony" John 4:39.

Among people to whom the Holy Spirit guides you

See Philip in Acts 8:26-36.

To the whole world

See Mark 16:15.

The worth of a soul

"The salvation of one soul is worth more than the framing of a Magna Carta of a thousand worlds." *John Keble*

How can I give my testimony?

First things first

Now the first thing to say about "how should I give my testimony?" is that this is a bad question. It is, strictly speaking, to talk about "me/I" and "my" testimony. We all know what is meant by this. But it is crucial that any testimony about Jesus, not least of all when it is in public, should be about what Jesus has done for me, rather than about me and what happened to me.

Pray

Ask the Lord Jesus to give you his wisdom for this.

Length

If you're asked to say a few words about how you became a Christian, don't think of a long sermon, think of just three minutes.

Write it out

If this is the first time you are going to do this don't think that the Holy Spirit can only guide you if stand up and speak totally unprepared. When Jesus promised that his disciples would be given words to speak and that they shouldn't worry about what to say because the Holy Spirit would tell them, he was referring to a totally different situation. He was talking about his disciples being hauled before aggressive synagogues and rulers. See Luke 12:11, 12.

If you write out what you are going to say you can learn it by heart. Also you can time yourself, to make sure that it's the right length. On top of that you can have it to hand when you are speaking, in case you want to refer to it or even read from it.

Ingredients

1. Say a word about how you were before you became a Christian.
2. Say a word about what first, or finally, attracted you to Jesus.
3. Say a word about any struggles you had about trusting in Jesus.
4. Say a word about how you "found" Jesus, "asked Jesus into your life," or whatever expression you find helpful to use about the time when you became a Christian. Don't worry if you did not have a conversion experience like Paul did on the Damascus Road. There are some exceedingly strong and mature Christians who were brought up in Christian homes who will tell you that they never knew a time when they did not know Jesus as their Friend and Savior.

Don't exaggerate

Some people feel that their testimonies are rather puny in comparison with those you read about in magazines and books. Don't worry about that. Many people put their faith in Jesus in a very quiet, low key, way.

Pitfalls to avoid

1. Try to avoid saying anything negative about anyone or any organization.
2. Try and speak in ordinary language.
3. Try to avoid religious jargon.
4. Try to avoid talking about any sensational sin, but rather speak about how wonderful Jesus is to you. Some of the things included in so-called Christian testimonies would be barred by the film censors!

Things to include

1. If a particular verse from the Bible helped you, mention it.
2. Don't let everything be in the past tense. Think about ending with a way that you are helped today by Jesus.

Writing style

As you start to write imagine that there is someone in the room with you. Think how you would tell that person about what you are trying to write down. Try to make what you write down have a conversational style to it.

Read what you've written

Read through what you've written. Ask yourself: Does it all make sense? Edit, reshape anything that sounds funny.

Pray and pray again

Pray just before you speak. Pray as soon as you have finished speaking.

Thank Jesus for all the help you have received in this.

How to win souls for Christ

Introducing C. H. Spurgeon

For more than forty years, Charles Haddon Spurgeon, 1834–1892, a Baptist preacher, was, through his preaching, through his private conversations with individuals, and through his writing, one of the greatest soul-winners of his age. What follows concerns what Spurgeon wrote about what he called "the chief business of all Christians, including the Christian minister."

This edited version of his sermon retains Spurgeon's original language and his use of the *King James Version* of the Bible.

What is it to win a soul?

Concerning the winning of souls. What is it to win a soul? I hope you believe in the old-fashioned way of saving souls. We all believe that we must go to soul-winning, desiring in God's name to see all things made new. In the process of our work, we endeavor to bless men by trying to make them temperate; may God bless all work of that sort! But we should think ourselves to have failed if we had produced a world of total abstainers, and had left them all unbelievers. We drive at something more than temperance; for we believe that men must be born again.

The need for spiritual life

But that is not so much our work as this: that the dead in sin should live, that spiritual life should quicken them, and that Christ should reign where the prince of the power of the air now hath sway. You preach, brethren, with this object, that men may quit their sins, and fly to Christ for pardon, that by His blessed Spirit they may be renovated, and become as much in love with everything that is holy as they are now in love with everything that is sinful. You aim at a radical cure; the ax is laid at the root of the trees; the amendment of the old nature would not content you, but you seek for the imparting, by a divine power, of a new nature, that those who gather round you in the streets may live unto God.

We aim for miracles
Our object is to turn the world upside down; or, in other words, that where sin abounded grace may much more abound. We are aiming at a miracle: it is well to settle that at the commencement. Some brethren think that they ought to lower their note to the spiritual ability of the hearer; but this is a mistake. According to these brethren, you ought not to exhort a man to repent and believe unless you believe that he can, of himself, repent and believe. My reply is a confession: I command men in the name of Jesus to repent and believe the gospel, though I know they can do nothing of the kind apart from the grace of God; for I am not sent to work according to what my private reason might suggest, but according to the orders of my Lord

and Master.

Ours is the miraculous method which comes of the endowment of the Spirit of God, who bids His ministers perform wonders in the name of the holy child Jesus. We are sent to say to blind eyes, "See," to deaf ears, "Hear," to dead hearts, "Live." Dare we do this? We shall be wise to begin with the conviction that we are utterly powerless for this unless our Master has sent us, and is with us. But if He that sent us is with us, all things are possible to him that believeth. There is no limit to what God can accomplish if He works by thy heart and voice.

Instruments in God's hands
The other Sabbath morning, before I entered the pulpit, when my dear brethren, the deacons and elders of this church, gathered about me for prayer, one of them said, "Lord, take him as a man takes a tool in his hand when he gets a firm hold of it, and then uses it to work his own will with it." That is what all workers need; that God may be the Worker by them. You are to be instruments in the hands of God; yourselves, of course, actively putting forth all your faculties and forces which the Lord has lent to you; but still never depending upon your personal power, but resting alone upon that sacred, mysterious, divine energy which worketh in us, and by us, and with us, upon the hearts and minds of men.

Our converts, or the Lord's converts?

Brethren, we have been greatly disappointed, have we not, with some of our converts? We shall always be disappointed with them so far as they are *our* converts. We shall greatly rejoice over them when they prove to be the Lord's work.

It is not our way of putting the gospel, nor our method of illustrating it, which wins souls, but the gospel itself does the work in the hands of the Holy Ghost, and to Him we must look for the thorough conversion of men. We go in, then, for thorough downright conversion; and therefore we fall back upon the power of the Holy Spirit. If it be a miracle, God must work it, that is clear; it is not to be accomplished by our reasoning, or persuasion, or threatening, it can only come from the Lord.

The Spirit of God

In what way, since the winning of souls lies here, can we hopefully expect to be endowed with the Spirit of God, and to go forth in His power?

I reply, that a great deal depends upon the condition of the man himself. I am persuaded we have never laid enough stress on the work of God within our own selves in its relation to our service of God. A consecrated man may be charged with the divine energy to the full, so that everybody round about him must

perceive it. At another time that same person may be feeble and dull. Dear brethren, look carefully to your own condition before God. Take care of the home farm; look well to your own flocks and herds. Unless your walk be close with God, unless you dwell in that clear light which surrounds the throne of God, and which is only known to those who are in fellowship with the Eternal, you will go forth from your chamber, and hasten to your work, but nothing will come of it. Let me show you some ways in which much must depend in soul-winning upon the man himself.

We must be witnesses

We win some souls to Christ by acting as witnesses. We stand up and testify for the Lord Jesus Christ concerning certain truths. Now, I have never had the great privilege of being bamboozled by a barrister. I have sometimes wondered what I should do if I were put into the witness-box to be examined and cross-examined. I think I should simply stand up, and tell the truth as far as I knew it, and should not make an attempt to display my wit, or my language, or my judgment. If I simply gave straightforward answers to his questions, I should beat any lawyer under heaven. But the difficulty is, that so often when a witness is put into the box, he is more conscious of himself than of what he has to say;

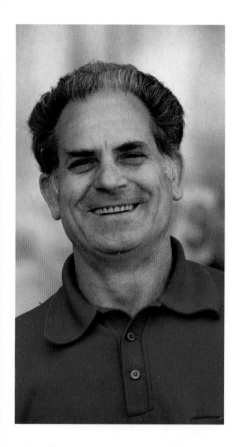

since, if you are not saved yourself, you yet wish others to be. You do not doubt that you once enjoyed full assurance; and now, if you have sorrowfully to confess, "Alas! I do not feel the full power of the gospel on my own heart," you can truly add, "Yet I know that it is true, for I have seen it save others, and I know that no other power can save me." Perhaps even that faltering testimony, so truly honest, might bring a tear into your opponent's eye, and make him feel sympathy for you.

"I preached," said John Bunyan, "sometimes without hope, like a man in chains to men in chains, and when I heard my own fetters rattle, yet I told others that there was deliverance for them, and I bade them look to the great Deliverer." I would not have stopped Mr. Bunyan in preaching so. At the same time, it is a great thing to be able to declare from your own personal experience that the Lord hath broken the gates of brass, and cut through the bars of iron.

I preach what I know

A man ought to know what he is preaching about, or else let him sit down. If I had any doubt about the matters I preach from this pulpit, I should be ashamed to remain the pastor of this church; but I preach what I do know, and testify what I have seen. If I am mistaken, I am heartily and intensely mistaken; and I

therefore, he is soon worried, teased, and bored, and, by losing his temper, he fails to be a good witness for the cause.

The witness must be saved

Brethren, the witnessing man, then, must himself be saved, and he should be sure of it. I do not know whether you doubt your own salvation. Perhaps I should recommend you to preach even when that is the case;

risk my soul and all its eternal interests upon the truth of what I preach. If the gospel which I preach does not save me, I shall never be saved, for what I proclaim to others is my own personal ground of trust. I have no private lifeboat; the ark to which I invite others holds myself and all that I have.

We must be pleaders

But you are not only witnesses, you are pleaders for the Lord Jesus Christ. Now, in a pleader, much depends upon the man. It seems as if the sign and token of Christianity in some preachers was not a tongue of fire, but a block of ice. You would not like to have a barrister stand up and plead your cause in a cool, deliberate way, never showing the slightest care about whether you were found guilty of murder or acquitted. How could you endure his indifference when you yourself were likely to be hanged? Oh, no! you wish to silence such a false advocate. So, when a man has to speak for Christ, if he is not in earnest, let him go to bed. Do let us all learn the art of pleading with the souls of men.

We must be examples

Still, we have not only to be witnesses and pleaders, but we have also to be examples. One of the most successful ways of taking wild ducks is the use of the decoy bird. The decoy duck enters

the net itself, and the others follow it. We need to use more, in the Christian Church, the holy art of decoy; that is to say, our example, in ourselves coming to Christ, in ourselves living godly lives in the midst of a perverse generation, our example of joy and sorrow, our example of holy submission to the divine will in the time of trouble, our example in all manner of gracious ways, will be the means of inducing others to enter the way of life.

Seek help from a fellow-Christian

It is a very great assistance to join in brotherly league with some warm-hearted Christian who knows more than we do, and will benefit us by prudent hints. God may bless us for the sake of others when He might not bless us for our own. You have heard, I daresay, the monkish story of the man who had preached, and had won many souls to Christ, and congratulated himself upon it.

One night, it was revealed to him that he should have none of the honor of it at the last great day; and he asked the angel in his dream who then would have the credit of it, and the angel replied, "That deaf old man who sits on the pulpit stairs, and prays for you, was the means of the blessing." Let us be thankful for that deaf man, or, that old woman, or those poor praying friends who bring down a blessing upon us by their intercessions. The

Spirit of God will bless two when He might not bless one.

Hard work

Dear brethren, if we are going to win souls, we must go in for downright labor and hard work.

Work at your preaching

And, first, we must work at our preaching. Go on with your preaching. Cobbler, stick to your last; preacher, stick to your preaching. In the great day, when the muster-roll shall be read, of all those who are converted through fine music, and church decoration, and religious exhibitions and entertainments, they will amount to the tenth part of nothing; but it will always please God by the foolishness of preaching to save them that believe. Keep to your preaching; and if you do anything beside, do not let it throw your preaching into the background. In the first place preach, and in the second place preach, and in the third place preach.

God's way is by preaching

- Believe in preaching the love of Christ,
- believe in preaching the atoning sacrifice,
- believe in preaching the new birth,
- believe in preaching the whole counsel of God.

The old hammer of the gospel will still break the rock in pieces; the ancient fire of Pentecost will still burn among the multitude. Try nothing new, but go on with preaching, and if we all preach with the Holy Ghost sent down from heaven, the results of preaching will astound us.

If the Lord's own way of mercy fails, then hang the skies in mourning, and blot out the sun in everlasting midnight, for there remaineth nothing before our race but the blackness of darkness. Salvation by the sacrifice of

Jesus is the ultimatum of God. Rejoice that it cannot fail. Let us believe without reserve, and then go straight ahead with the preaching of the Word.

Talking to an individual
Last Sunday night, my dear brother told us a little story which I shall never forget. He was at Croydon Hospital one night, as one of those appointed to visit it. All the porters had gone home, and it was time to shut up for the night. He was the only person in the hospital, with the exception of the physician, when a boy came running in, saying that there was a railway accident, and someone must go round to the station with a stretcher. The doctor said to my brother, "Will you take one end of the stretcher if I take the other?"

"Oh, yes!" was the cheerful reply; and so away went the doctor and the pastor with the stretcher. They brought a sick man back with them. My brother said, "I went often to the hospital during the next week or two, because I felt so much interest in the man whom I had helped to carry." I believe he will always take an interest in that man, because he once felt the weight of him. It should be the same for us as we talk with individuals about our Lord. When you know how to carry a man on your heart, and have felt the burden of his case, you will have his name engraved upon your soul.

Make use of tracts
When preaching and private talk are not available, have a tract ready. Some tracts would not convert a beetle: there is not enough in them to interest a fly. Get good striking tracts, or none at all. But a telling, touching gospel tract may often be the seed of eternal life; therefore, do not go out without your tracts.

Be in earnest
We are not half as earnest as we ought to be. Do you not remember the young man, who, when he was dying, said to his brother, "My brother, how could you have been so indifferent to my soul as you have been?"

He answered, "I have not been indifferent to your soul, for I have frequently spoken to you about it."

"Oh, yes!" he said, "you spoke; but somehow, I think, if you had remembered that I was going down to hell, you would have been more earnest with me; you would have wept over me, and, as my brother, you would not have allowed me to be lost."

Let no one say this of you.

As Hannibal is said to have melted the rocks with vinegar, so earnestness will one way or another dissolve the rocky hearts of men. May the Spirit of God rest upon you, one and all, for Jesus Christ's sake! Amen.

C. H. Spurgeon

The wordless book

Do you believe in child evangelism?

Polycarp, 95–155, bishop of Smyrna, was converted at the age of nine.

Matthew Henry, the great Bible commentator, was converted at the age of 11.

Isaac Watts, writer of so many much-loved hymns, was converted at the age of seven.

According to some polls, do you know at what age most people become Christians? Over 75% of people accept Christ between the ages of 8 and 14.

What is the wordless book?

The wordless book is a book of colored pages which is used in leading children to Jesus. It consists of no words, but has the following colored double pages:

- a dark page
- a red page
- a clean page
- a green page
- a gold page.

How to use the wordless book

It's up to you how you talk about this book with children. What follows are just the topics that you need to cover.

Talking with children about Jesus is a very great privilege and a grave responsibility. Don't force children into making a decision for Jesus. Remember

that some children like to give adults the answers they think they want to hear, rather than the answers they really believe.

Make sure that you know the name of the child you are speaking to, and use it all the time as you go through the wordless book.

Be pleasant and happy. Smile, rather than have a grim, poker face.

Starting

Ask (let's call the child's name Robert[a]) Robert[a] if he/she has ever seen a book without words or pictures before.

Flick through the book quickly so the colors are seen.

Say that this book, even though it has no words, tells a true story from the Bible.

The gold pages

Ask if Robert[a] has ever had a look at the end of a book to see how the story ends. Say that this is how we're going to start with this book.

Turn to the last double page, the gold pages.

(The point about starting with the gold pages is that it means you have the opportunity of talking about Jesus' love. However, you may prefer to start with the dark pages, and leave turning to the gold pages until the end.)

One way of going through the wordless book is to say everything in the first person. So you could say at this point: "These gold pages remind me of heaven."

Then say how heaven is God's home… that it is a wonderful place…where nobody is ever ill…where nobody ever dies…where there is no night…where everyone is really happy.

The best think thing about heaven is that Jesus is there.

God made the whole world…God make each person in the world…and Jesus loves everyone in the world, including you and me. And Jesus wants us to live with him in heaven.

The one thing that is not in heaven is anything that is bad or wrong or evil.

The dark pages

Turn to the front of the book, to the dark double pages.

These dark pages remind me of my sin, and all the times when I have not pleased the Lord Jesus.

They make me think of the things I have done which are wrong.

These pages make me remember the thoughts I have thought which have made Jesus sad.

They tell me that I have not loved Jesus with all my heart.

They show me that my badness and sin are like a barrier between me and God.

They help me to understand that I am cut off from God.

The red pages

These red pages show me the way I can be close to Jesus.

They are red to remind me that Jesus died for me when he was put to death on the cross.

At this point you could use the illustration found on page 120 of this book about how our sin is taken off us and put on Jesus at Jesus' crucifixion.

These pages remind me about how much Jesus loves me. That he loves me so much that he has taken my badness and sin on him.

I love these pages because they tell me that I can now be Jesus' close friend.

The clean pages

These pages remind me that Jesus can forgive me and make me clean.

You could use the verse from Revelation 3:20 with the picture by Holman Hunt here, which is explained on page 121 of this book.

The thank you prayer

If you think it right to encourage Robert[a] to ask Jesus into his/her life now, suggest that they follow a thank you prayer you are going to pray aloud, but that they say it without speaking out aloud.

Or, you may like to suggest that you are going to say this thank you prayer line by line twice. And that the second time Robert[a] can say it in his/her heart as you repeat it.

Keep this prayer simple.

It could be:

"Dear Lord Jesus, (repeat)

thank you, (repeat)
for all your love for me, (repeat)
Thank you, (repeat)
for dying on the cross, (repeat)
to take away my sin, (repeat)
Please come, (repeat)
into my life now, (repeat)
Amen. (repeat)

The green pages

These green pages are meant to stand for spiritual growth.

The link with green being that green grass grows, as do flowers and trees with their green leaves.

They remind me that I have to grow, as a baby grows into a child, and as a child grows into an adult.

They also remind me that I have to grow strong as Jesus' friend.

I know that I can grow in this way by reading my Bible and by talking with the Lord Jesus in prayer.

These green pages give you the opportunity to do any of the following things. Just do what you think is appropriate and feasible.

- Give a children's tract.
- Gve the wordless book.
- Give the Holman Hunt picture.
- Take an address. Be ultra sensitive here. Parents, rightly, may not be happy to think that a stranger (if that is what you are) has the name and address of their child.
- Remember that some homes are very anti-Christian.

• Work out how Robert[a] can be linked up to a children's group at his/her church.

Pray

Pray, especially over the next seven days, for Robert[a]. This is the most-important thing you can do.

The story behind the wordless book

It's been in existence for over 100 years and is used today by a number of Christian organizations which specialize in child evangelism. It is still used widely today.

C. H. Spurgeon

In 1866, when the wordless book only had three pages double pages, black, red and white, Charles Spurgeon preached a sermon entitled "The Wordless Book," at the Metropolitan Tabernacle in London.

During this sermon Spurgeon said how an old unnamed minister put three pages together and often looked at them to remind himself of his sinfulness, of Christ's blood poured out for him, and of the wonder of Jesus' forgiveness and cleansing of his sins.

Spurgeon then told his adult congregation: "I want you, dear friends, to read this book this evening....may God the Holy Spirit help us do so to our profit."

Added pages

The gold pages were added later to depict the wonder of heaven. In 1875 D. L. Moody used it with the gold pages.

Blind Fanny Crosby, the author of the hymn *Blessed Assurance*, kept a wordless book in her purse and often told its story to children.

In 1939 the Child Evangelism Fellowship published the wordless book with the green pages, representing Christian growth, added.

The best Bible texts for those who have difficulties

HELPING PEOPLE WITH GENUINE DIFFICULTIES

Here are 12 of the most common objections which are put forward against becoming a Christian, with relevant Bible verses.

	Objection	Key verse	Other verses
1.	"I am too great a sinner."	Here is a trustworthy saying that deserves full acceptance: Christ Jesus came into the world to save sinners – of whom I am the worst." *1 Timothy 1:15*	Romans 5:6, 8 Isaiah 1:18 John 6:37
2.	"I must be a better person before I become a Christian."	"It is not the healthy who need a doctor, but the sick...For I have not come to call the righteous, but sinners." *Matthew 9:12, 13*	Luke 19:10 Luke 15:18, 20-24 Luke 18:10-14
3.	"I am afraid that I may fail, if I try."	"I give them eternal life, and they shall never perish; no one can snatch them out of my hand. My Father, who has given them to me, is greater than all, no one can snatch them out of my Father's hand." *John 10:28, 29*	Isaiah 41:10, 13 1 Peter 1:5 2 Timothy 1:12 Jude 24, 25 1 Corinthians 10:13
4.	"But I am so weak."	"I can do all things through him who gives me strength." *Philippians 4:13*	2 Corinthians 12:9, 10
5.	"I have tried before and failed."	"Simon, Simon, Satan has asked to sift you as wheat. But I have prayed for you, Simon, that your faith may not fail. And when you have turned back, strengthen your brothers." *Luke 22:31, 32*	Romans 8:3, 4 Isaiah 40:29-31 1 John 5:4 1 Peter 5:6-10
6.	"I can't give up my evil ways."	"Do not be deceived: God cannot be mocked. A man reaps what he sows. The one who sows to please his sinful nature, from that nature will reap destruction; the one who sows to please the Spirit, from the Spirit will reap eternal life." *Galatians 6:7, 8*	John 8:36
7.	"I have too much to give up."	"What good is it for a man to gain the whole world, yet forfeit his soul?" *Mark 8:36*	Romans 8:32 1 John 2:15-17 Hebrews 11:24-26

8.	"I am afraid of being made fun of/persecution."	"If anyone is ashamed of me and my words in this adulterous and sinful generation, the Son of Man will be ashamed of him when he comes in his Father's glory with the holy angels." *Mark 8:38*	Proverbs 29:25
9.	"I have committed the unpardonable sin."	Explain what the unpardonable sin is. "And so I tell you, every sin and blasphemy will be forgiven men, but the blasphemy against the Spirit will not be forgiven. Anyone who speaks a word against the Son of Man will be forgiven, but anyone who speak against the Holy Spirit will not be forgiven, either in this age or in the age to come." *Matthew 12:31, 32* Explain that the following verses describes one who "falls away," that is, becomes an apostate, renounces Christianity. It does not describe one who merely falls into sin, even deep sin, as Peter the apostle did. "It is impossible for those who have once been enlightened, who have tasted the heavenly gift, who have shared in the Holy Spirit, who have tasted the goodness of the word of God and the powers of the coming age, if they fall away, to be brought back to repentance, because to their loss they are crucifying the Son of God all over again and subjecting him to public disgrace." *Hebrews 6:4-6*	
10.	"Christians are so inconsistent. There are so many hypocrites who go to church."	"So then, each of us will give an account to himself to God." *Romans 14:12*	Romans 2:1-5 Matthew 7:1-5
11.	"God seems to me to be unjust and cruel."	"But who are you, O man, to talk back to God? 'Shall what is formed say to him who formed it, "Why did you make me like this?"'" *Romans 9:20*	Romans 11:33 Isaiah 55:8-9 Hebrews 12:5-7, 10-12
12.	"There is someone I can't forgive."	"But if you do not forgive men their sins, your Father will not forgive your sins." *Matthew 6:15*	Matthew 18:23-25 Ephesians 4:32 Galatians 5:22, 23

The best Bible texts for skeptics

	HELPING SKEPTICS		
	Here are seven common objections which are put forward against believing in God and in Jesus, with relevant Bible verses.
	Objection	*Key verse*	*Other verses*
1.	"It's not true."	[Luke claimed that his Gospel was based on eyewitness reports.] "Many have undertaken to draw up an account of the things that have been fulfilled among us, just as they were handed down to us by those who from the first were eye-witnesses and servants of the word." *Luke 1:1, 2*	Acts 1:1-3
2.	"You can't trust a book written by enthusiasts."	"Therefore, since I myself have carefully investigated everything from the beginning, it seemed good to me to write an orderly account for you, most excellent Theophilus, so that you may know the certainty of the things you have been taught." *Luke 1:3, 4*	Acts 24:1-21
3.	"The Bible is not historically accurate."	"In those days Caesar Augustus issued a decree that a census should be taken of the entire Roman world. (This was the first census that took place while Quirinius was governor of Syria)." *Luke 2:1, 2*	Acts 23:23-26
4.	"The message of the Bible is out of date."	[God does not change, nor does humankind's need for salvation change.] "Jesus Christ is the same yesterday and today and for ever." *Hebrews 13:8*	Romans 3:23
5.	"Christianity does not turn me on."	[God has only provided one way of salvation, whether we like it or not.] "Salvation is found in no one else, [other than Jesus Christ], for there is no other name under heaven given to men by which we must be saved." *Acts 4:12*	Acts 10:43
6.	"I'm happy with my own beliefs."	[It's not a matter of how you feel about what you believe, it's a question of the truth.] "Jesus answered, 'I am the way and the truth and the life. No one comes to the Father except through me.'" *John 14:6*	John 8:32, 36
7.	"I don't even believe in God."	[The Bible never attempts to prove the existence of God, but rather assumes his existence. It calls people who don't believe in God "fools".] "The fool says in his heart, 'There is no God.'" *Psalm 14:1*	John 20:30, 31

The best Bible texts for those who make excuses

Excuses, excuses, excuses

There is nothing new in people making excuses about why they do not want to follow Jesus. Jesus himself met many such people.

Such people need to be confronted with the Word of God. The worst thing you can do when talking with people who are making such excuses is to get angry with them. Try to point them to what the Bible says about them, and do not get involved in a slanging match.

ANSWERING COMMON EXCUSES			
Here are six common excuses which are put forward for not believing in God and in Jesus, with relevant Bible verses.			
	Excuse	*Key verse*	*Other verses*
1.	"I'll be okey because God is a God of love."	"Then the king told the attendants, 'Tie him hand and foot, and throw him outside, into the darkness, where there will be weeping and gnashing of teeth.'" *Matthew 22:13*	Luke 13:3
2.	"I don't want to leave my friends."	"Do not be yoked together with unbelievers. For what do righteousness and wickedness have in common? Or what fellowship can light have with darkness?" *2 Corinthians 6:14*	1 Corinthians 15:33
3.	"I've tried this before."	"To him who is able to keep you from falling and to present you before his glorious presence without fault and with great joy." *Jude 24*	Hebrews 7:25
4.	"It's too late for me."	"And if a wicked man turns away from his wickedness and does what is just and right, he will live by doing so." *Ezekiel 33:19*	John 6:37; Luke 23:43
5.	"Not today, thank you."	"Seek the Lord while he may be found; call on him while he is near." *Isaiah 55:6*	Matthew 24:44; Joshua 24:15; Luke 12:19, 20
6.	"I have too many problems with belief."	"The secret things belong to the Lord our God, but the things revealed belong to us and to our children for ever, that we may follow all the words of this law." *Deuteronomy 29:29*	1 Corinthians 13:12

The best Bible texts for Spiritualists, the nominally religious and Jehovah's Witnesses

THE BEST BIBLE TEXTS FOR SPIRITUALISTS			
	Topic	*Key verse*	*Other verses*
1.	Mediums should not be consulted.	"When men tell you to consult mediums and spiritists, who whisper and mutter, should not a people enquire of their God? Why consult the dead on behalf of the living? To the law and to the testimony! If they do not speak according to this word, they have no light of dawn." *Isaiah 8:19-20*	Leviticus 19:31; 20:6; Deuteronomy 18:10-12; 1 John 4:1, 3; 2 Thessalonians 2:9-12; 1 Chronicles 10:13, 14; 2 Kings 21:1, 2, 6

THE BEST BIBLE TEXTS FOR THE NOMINALLY RELIGIOUS			
	Topic	*Key verse*	*Other verses*
1.	The necessity of new birth.	"In reply Jesus declared, 'I tell you the truth, unless a man is born again, he cannot see the kingdom of God.'…Jesus answered, 'I tell you the truth, unless a man is born of water and the Spirit, he cannot enter the kingdom of God…You should not be surprised at my saying, "You must be born again."'" *John 3:3, 5, 7*	1 John 2:29; 1 Peter 2:1, 2
2.	Jesus is the only mediator.	"For there is one God and one mediator between God and men, the man Christ Jesus." *1 Timothy 2:5*	Acts 13:39

THE BEST BIBLE TEXTS FOR JEHOVAH'S WITNESSES

	Topic	Key verse	Other verses
1.	The Bible is God's revelation.	"Above all you must understand that no prophecy of Scripture came about by the prophet's own interpretation. For prophecy never had its origin in the will of man, but men spoke from God as they were carried along by the Holy Spirit." *2 Peter 1:20, 21*	2 Timothy 3:14-17; Revelation 22:18, 19
2.	Jesus is God.	"Dear friends, do not believe every spirit, but test the spirits to see whether they are from God, because many false prophets have gone out into the world. This is how you can recognize the Spirit of God: Every spirit that acknowledges that Jesus Christ has come in the flesh is from God, but every spirit that does not acknowledge Jesus is not from God. This is the spirit of the antichrist, which you have heard is coming and even now is already in the world." *1 John 4:1-3*	Colossians 2:9; Exodus 3:14; John 8:58; John 1:1, 2, 14; Matthew 11:27
3.	We are all accountable to God.	"The soul who sins is the one who will die. The son will not share the guilt of the father, nor will the father share the guilt of the son. The righteousness of the righteous man will be credited to him, and the wickedness of the wicked will be charged against him." *Ezekiel 18:20*	Romans 14:11, 12; 6:23
4.	Eternal life and atonement only come through Jesus.	"For what I received I passed on to you as of first importance: that Christ died for our sins according to the Scriptures, that he was buried, that he was raised on the third day according to the Scriptures." *1 Corinthians 15:3, 4*	Isaiah 53:5, 6, 10; Zechariah 13:1; 1 Timothy 1:15, 16; 1 John 1:7-9; Romans 5:6, 8; John 10:27-30
5.	Salvation comes through faith, not by good deeds.	"For by grace you have been saved, through faith–and this not from yourselves, it is the gift of God–not by works, so that no one can boast." *Ephesians 2:8, 9*	Romans 1:17; 4:2, 3; John 6:28, 29
6.	Our future state is certain.	"Do not be amazed at this, for a time is coming when all who are in their graves will hear his voice and come out–those who have done good will rise to live, and those who have done evil will rise to be condemned." *John 5:28, 29*	2 Thessalonians 1:7-10; Luke 16:25, 26; Mark 9:43; Revelation 20:14, 15; 21:6-8

The best Bible texts for Mormons and Jews

	THE BEST BIBLE TEXTS FOR MORMONS		
	Theme	*Key verse*	*Other verses*
1.	There is only one God, who is separate from humankind.	"For I am God, and not man–the Holy One among you." *Hosea 11:9*	Isaiah 42:8; 44:6-8
2.	Jesus is the only Savior.	"Salvation is found in on one else [other than Jesus Christ of Nazareth], for there is no other name under heaven given to men by which we must be saved." *Acts 4:12*	John 3:16; Galatians 1:3, 4
3.	Humankind is sinful.	"There is not a righteous man on earth who does what is right and never sins." *Ecclesiastes 7:20*	Romans 3:22-24; 5:12; 3:11, 12
4.	Salvation comes through faith, not through good deeds.	"But when the kindness and love of God our Savior appeared, he saved us, not because of righteous things we had done, but because of his mercy." *Titus 3:4, 5*	Romans 1:17; John 6:28, 29; Galatians 3:10, 11; Ephesians 2:8, 9
5.	All Christians belong to God's priesthood now.	"As you come to him, the living Stone –rejected by men but chosen by God and precious to him–you also, like living stones, are being built into a spiritual house to be a holy priesthood, offering spiritual sacrifices acceptable to God through Jesus Christ." *1 Peter 2:4, 5*	
6.	Jesus is the mediator for Christians.	"This is good and pleases God our Savior, who wants all men to be saved and to come to a knowledge of the truth. For there is one God and one mediator between God and men, the man Christ Jesus, who gave himself as a ransom for all men–the testimony given in its proper place." *1 Timothy: 3-6*	

	THE BEST BIBLE TEXT FOR JEWS		
	Theme	*Key verse*	*Other verses*
1.	Jesus is the long awaited Messiah, Savior, and suffering servant.	"She will give birth to a son, and you are to give him the name Jesus, because he will save his people from their sins." *Matthew 1:21*	Isaiah 52:13–53:12

The best Bible texts for those who want to become followers of Jesus

	THE BEST BIBLE TEXTS FOR GENUINE SEEKERS		
	Theme	*Key verse*	*Other verses*
1.	Jesus bears our sins.	"He himself bore our sins in his body on the tree [cross], so that we might die to sins and live for righteousness; by his wounds you have been healed." *1 Peter 2:24*	Isaiah 53:6; 2 Corinthians 3:13; 1 John 4:10; 2:2; Colossians 1:19, 20; Ephesians 1:7; Romans 5:6-11
2.	The risen Jesus has broken the power of sin.	"For what I received I passed on to you as of first importance: that Christ died for our sins according to the Scriptures, that he was buried, that he was raised on the third day according to the Scriptures." *1 Corinthians 15:3, 4*	Matthew 28:18, 20; 1:21; Romans 7:20, 21, 23-25; Jude 24, 25; Isaiah 41:10, 13; 1 Peter 1:5; Philippians 4:13
3.	Jesus is alive now, praying for us.	"Therefore he is able to save completely those who come to God through him, because he always lives to intercede for them." *Hebrews 7:25*	1 John 2:1; Romans 8:34
4.	To have Jesus as their Savior they have to believe on him, that is receive him.	"Declare what is to be, present it–let them take counsel together. Who foretold this long ago, who declared it from the distant past? Was it not I, the Lord? And there is no God apart from me, a righteous God and a Savior; there is none but me. Turn to me and be saved, all you ends of the earth, for I am God, and there is no other." *Isaiah 45:21, 22*	John 1:12; 3:16, 36; Acts 16:31; 10:43; 13:39

The best Bible texts for people involved in the cults

THE BEST BIBLE TEXTS FOR THOSE INVOLVED IN CULTS BASED ON WESTERN RELIGIONS		
	Theme	*Key text*
1.	The Holy Spirit is God.	"But God has revealed it to us by his Spirit. The Spirit searches all things, even the deep things of God. For who among men knows the thoughts of a man except the man's spirit within him? In the same way no one knows the thoughts of God except the Spirit of God. We have not received the spirit of the world but the Spirit who is from God, that we may understand what God has freely given us." *1 Corinthians 2:10-12*
2.	Jesus is God.	"In the past God spoke to our forefathers through the prophets at many times and in various ways, but in these last days he has spoken to us by his Son, whom he appointed heir of all things, and through whom he made the universe." *Hebrews 1:1, 2*
3.	Jesus succeeded in his mission on earth.	"Christ was sacrificed once to take away the sins of many people; and he will appear a second time, not to bear sin, but to bring salvation to those who are waiting for him." *Hebrews 9:28*

	THE BEST BIBLE TEXTS FOR THOSE INVOLVED IN EASTERN CULTS AND EASTERN RELIGIONS		
	Theme	*Key verse*	*Other verses*
1.	God is the Creator God, but is separate from his creation.	"In the beginning God created the heavens and the earth." *Genesis 1:1*	
2.	God and Jesus have always existed and were not created.	"In the beginning was the Word, and the Word was with God, and the Word was God. He was with God in the beginning. Through him all things were made, without him nothing was made that was made." *John 1:1-3*	
3.	Only faith in Jesus enables a person to link up with God.	"The righteousness from God comes through faith in Jesus Christ to all who believe. There is no difference, for all have sinned and fall short of the glory of God." *Romans 3:22, 23*	
4.	For people involved in Transcendental Meditation: humankind's problem is ignorance of God.	"There is no one righteous, not even one; there is no one who understands, no one who seeks God. All have turned away, they have together become worthless, there is no one who does good, not even one." *Romans 3:11, 12*	
5.	For people involved in Transcendental Meditation: peace comes from serving God.	"But seek first his [God's] kingdom and his righteousness, and all these things will be given to you as well." *Matthew 6:33*	Matthew 5:6
6.	For those who believe in reincarnation.	"Man is destined to die once, and after that to face judgment." *Hebrews 9:27*	John 5:28, 29
7.	Jesus is a perfect and blameless Savior.	"For we do not have a high priest who is unable to sympathize with our weaknesses, but we have one who has been tempted in every way, just as we are–yet without sin." *Hebrews 4:15*	Hebrews 7:26, 27

6

HOW TO BE A GOOD CHRISTIAN COUNSELOR

Introduction

In this chapter we turn from our own
problems to the difficulties faced by
other people. In these Old and New
Testament Bible studies, it's most
instructive to see the ways in which God
comforted his followers. We also look at
the examples and teaching of Paul and,
pre-eminently, Jesus.

A theologian was once defined as "a
man who spends his time answering
questions that nobody is asking." But
every Christian is a theologian. The only
question is: Are you a good or a bad
theologian? And the same goes for
Christian counseling. Whether they wish
it or not, all Christians are counselors to
one another. The spiritual principles
given in these studies are as relevant in
the twenty-first century as they were
when they were first written down by
the Bible writers. God, the God of all
comfort, has given us guidelines by
which we can be effective comforters if
we will only listen.

A strong Christian is a good counselor

The grace of God

We now move on from the last chapter where we thought about witnessing to non-Christians. That chapter could have been called "Counseling non-Christians." Now we consider how Christians are to counsel fellow-Christians.

As an introductory point we note that no Christian should ever counsel another Christian as if he or she were superior in any way. We are all saved sinners.

When the Protestant Reformer, John Bradford, who himself was later martyred, saw criminals being led away for execution, he said, "There, but for the grace of God, goes John Bradford." As we are saved by God's grace, so the only way to be a good Christian counselor is by God's grace.

A loving Christian will be a loving counselor

The best thing that a Christian can do if he/she desires to be a godly counselor is to be a godly Christian. When we ourselves need counseling, what we need most of all is God's love. The only way to be a loving counselor is to be a loving Christian.

We are loved by God

If we want to love other people in a Christian way we need to experience God's love for ourselves. Perhaps one of the most astounding statements Jesus made comes in John 15:9, where he tells his followers, "As the Father has loved me,

so have I loved you." That seems almost too incredible to be true. But it is true.

Ten things which cannot separate us from God's love

When Christians collapse they often blame a particular event in their lives, such as a bereavement, that has got them down. Paul writes to Christians at Rome, most of whom he had never met, about never being separated from God's love. In counseling God's love is the one thing we need to hang on to for ourselves, as well as mediate to the person we are seeking to help.

Here are the ten things that cannot separate us from God's love:

1. Death cannot separate us from the love of God: Romans 8:38.
2. Life cannot separate us from the love of God: Romans 8:38.
3. Angels cannot separate us from the love of God: Romans 8:38.
4. Demons cannot separate us from the love of God: Romans 8:38.
5. The present cannot separate us from the love of God: Romans 8:38.
6. The future cannot separate us from the love of God: Romans 8:38.
7. No powers can separate us from the love of God: Romans 8:38.
8. No height can separate us from the love of God: Romans 8:39.
9. No depth can separate us from the love of God: Romans 8:39.
10. Nothing in creation can separate us from the love of God: Romans 8:39.

Nine things that love is/does

As we reflect on God's great love for us we also realize what a responsibility we have to be loving.

1. Love is patient:
   1 Corinthians 13:4.
2. Love is kind: 1 Corinthians 13:5.
3. Love always protects:
   1 Corinthians 13:7.
4. Love always trusts:
   1 Corinthians 13:7.
5. Love always hopes:
   1 Corinthians 13:7.
6. Love always perseveres:
   1 Corinthians 13:7.
7. Love does not fade away, it remains:
   1 Corinthians 13:13.
8. Love covers a multitude of sins:
   1 Peter 4:8.
9. Perfect love drives out fear:
   1 John 4:18.

Four things that love is not

1. Love is not proud:
   1 Corinthians 13:4.
2. Love is not rude: 1 Corinthians 13:5.
3. Love is not self-seeking:
   1 Corinthians 13:5.
4. Love is not easily angered:
   1 Corinthians 13:5.

Six things that love does not do

1. Love does not envy:
   1 Corinthians 13:4.
2. Love does not boast:
   1 Corinthians 13:4.
3. Love does not keep any record of wrongs: 1 Corinthians 13:5.
4. Love does not delight in evil:
   1 Corinthians 13:6.
5. Love never fails: 1 Corinthians 13:8.
6. Love does no harm to its neighbor:
   Romans 13:10.

Where to find help in the Bible

The medicine cupboard

The Bible has been likened to a medicine cupboard where all different kinds of remedies are found. Some Christians dish out the same Bible verse in every situation. R. A. Torrey warned against this when he said: "There is a medicine in the Bible for every sin-sick soul, but every soul does not need the same medicine."

Key verses for our understanding about God

1. God is our shelter: Psalm 46:1-2.
2. It is possible to have peace in Jesus: John 16:33.
3. God looks at our hearts, not in the way people see us: 1 Samuel 16:7.
4. The Lord gives us joy: Psalm 126:2, 3.
5. Our salvation comes from what Jesus did: Titus 3:5, 6.
6. God tells us to believe in him: Isaiah 43:1.
7. If we look at Jesus we will see who God is like: Colossians 1:15-17.
8. The universe was not only created by God, it belongs to him: 1 Chronicles 29:11, 12.
9. All our spiritual needs are met in Jesus: Romans 8:32.

Key verses about Jesus and God

1. To know Jesus is to know God: John 8:19; 14:7.
2. To see Jesus is to see God: John 12:45; 14:9.
3. To believe in Jesus is to believe in God: John 12:44; 14:1.
4. To receive Jesus is to receive God: Mark 9:37.

5. To hate Jesus is to hate God:
John 15:23.
6. To honor Jesus is to honor God:
John 5:23.

**Key verses for our understanding about
our relationship to God**

1. We are loved by God: John 3:16.
2. Nothing need separate us from
God's love: Romans 8:38, 39.
3. Even after we are Christians we have
to confess our sins to God:
1 John 1:9.
4. When the Holy Spirit is in control of
our lives he makes us live fruitful
lives: Galatians 5:22.
5. God helps us when we are being
tempted: 1 Corinthians 10:13.
6. God promises to guide us:
Isaiah 58:11.
7. God wants us to walk in his ways:
Deuteronomy 10:12, 13.
8. God cares for those who love him:
Romans 8:28.
9. God's peace can protect our hearts:
Philippians 4:6, 7.
10. We are meant to be dedicated to
serving God: Romans 12:1.

**Key verses for our understanding about
our relationships with other people**

1. We are meant to love even our
enemies: Luke 6:25.
2. We should live our lives showing
love towards other people:
Ephesians 5:1, 2.
3. We should help the hungry and the
afflicted: Isaiah 58:10.
4. We should be glad to be hospitable
and pass on the blessings we have
received from God: 1 Peter 4:9, 10.
5. We should live in complete
harmony with other Christians:
Romans 15:5, 6.
6. We should speak healing words, not
wounding words: Proverbs 12:18.
7. We should respect our parents:
Deuteronomy 5:16.
8. In all our work we should work as if
we are working for the Lord, not as
if we are working for people:
Colossians 3:22-24.
9. We should be kind, humble, gentle,
patient, and forgiving:
Colossians 3:12, 13.
10. We should know how to reply if we
are asked about our Christian faith:
1 Peter 3:15, 16.

Weeping and rejoicing

Sympathy and empathy in abundance

Paul tells the Christians at Rome:
"Rejoice with those who rejoice; mourn
with those who mourn" Romans 12:15.

Principles of biblical counseling

The Bible sets out a number of clear
principles about how Christian pastors
are to look after their flock.

1. Find out what the difficulty, problem, or reason for rejoicing is

Paul is obviously saying that we tailor
our behavior to the mood of the person
we are seeking to help. Sometimes a
Christian counselor is so keen to impart
his "counseling" that he does not listen
properly and so does not even "hear"
what the person he is talking with is
saying.

Christian counselors should be
excellent listeners. Listening is a lost art.

"The first duty of love is to listen,"
Paul Tillich.

According to James 1:19 we should be
slow to speak, but quick to listen.

2. If necessary, ask a question

This is how Jesus helped people. Jesus
often answered a question with another
question, and did not answer the
original question he was asked. He did
this to help the person who was talking
to him to understand the situation he
was in.

Read through the Gospels and look
carefully at each section which records
somebody speaking to Jesus. A list of

examples of Jesus' conversations in
Matthew's Gospel is given in the next
section.

Note any of the following you can find
in each conversation.

a. Who is Jesus talking to?
b. Why did this person come to Jesus?
c. Did Jesus ask a question? If so, how
did it help the person Jesus was
speaking to.
d. How did the person leave Jesus? Did
he/she learn anything from the
conversation? If so, what?
e. Did Jesus tell the person to do
anything? If so, what?

Compile a list of good qualities that you
come across which will help you in your
Christian counseling. For example in
Matthew 10:16 Jesus tells his disciples
that they are to be:

• as shrewd as snakes, and
• as innocent as doves.

Matthew's Gospel

Study the following passages to see how
Jesus reacted in different situations and
how he spoke to people in various
circumstances.

• Matthew 3:13-17: Jesus meets John
the Baptist.
• Matthew 4:1-11: Jesus is tempted by
the devil.
• Matthew 4:17: Jesus preaches to the
crowds.
• Matthew 4:18-20: Jesus calls his first
disciples.

- Matthew 5–7: Jesus teaches his disciples (the Sermon on the Mount).
- Matthew 8:1-4: Jesus meets a man with leprosy.
- Matthew 8:5-13: Jesus meets a centurion.
- Matthew 8:18-22: Jesus speaks with a teacher of the law.
- Matthew 8:23-26: Jesus calms a storm.
- Matthew 9:1-8: Jesus meets a paralytic.
- Matthew 9:9-12: Jesus calls Matthew to follow him.
- Matthew 9:14-17: Jesus is asked a question about fasting.
- Matthew 9:18-21: Jesus heals a sick woman.
- Matthew 9:23-26: Jesus brings a dead girl back to life.
- Matthew 9:27-31: Jesus heals two blind men.
- Matthew 9:35-38: Jesus tells his disciples that the workers are few.
- Matthew 10:5-42: Jesus sends out his 12 disciples.
- Matthew 11:1-19: Jesus and John the Baptist's disciples.
- Matthew 11:20-24: Jesus and unrepentant cities.
- Matthew 11:25-30: Jesus speaks about rest for the weary.
- Matthew 12:1-14: Jesus speaks to Pharisees about the Sabbath.
- Matthew 12:22-37: Jesus speaks to Pharisees about Beelzebub.
- Matthew 12:38-45: Jesus speaks to Pharisees who seek a miraculous sign.
- Matthew 12:46-50: Jesus tells an un-named person who his mother and brothers are.
- Matthew 13:1-52: Jesus tells parables and answers his disciples' questions about them.
- Matthew 13:53-58: Jesus speaks with people from the synagogue in Nazareth.
- Matthew 14:13-21: Jesus feeds 5,000 people.
- Matthew 14:22-35: Jesus speaks to his disciples as he walks on the water.
- Matthew 15:1-20: Jesus answers Pharisees who accuse Jesus' disciples of eating with ceremonially unclean hands.
- Matthew 15:21-28: Jesus asks questions of a Canaanite woman.

Jesus our model

As in everything else in the Christian life, Jesus is the model for us when it comes to Christian counseling. It is worth completing the above studies in Matthew's Gospel and the other Gospels, even if it takes you many months.

The God of all comfort

One more principle of Christian counseling

Know the relevant teaching in the Bible to the problem a person has

While it is true that most people would make much better counselors if they said less and listened more, there does come a point when you do have to say something. You should be able to express your deep sympathy, if, for example, someone is facing bereavement. Somewhere along the line you should pray for an opportunity to point the person to some helpful teaching in the Bible. After you have gone the Bible verses you have suggested will be much more help than anything else.

Verses for Christians who have lost loved ones

It is hardly Christian to expect Christians not to be very deeply upset over the death of a loved one. While it is true that Paul once wrote that Christians should not grieve like other people do, see 1 Thessalonians 4:13, he meant there that they should not grieve like people who have no hope, no hope in the resurrection and the after-life. Like everyone else Christians need God's comfort in bereavement.

The following are passages that are appropriate at a time of bereavement.

- John 14:1-3, 27
- Psalm 46:10. This is just one verse and sometimes this is as much as a bereaved person can take in.

- 1 Thessalonians 4:13-18
- 2 Corinthians 5:6-8
- 1 Corinthians 15:42-44, 49, 53-58

Psalm 23

In a time of bereavement many people are greatly comforted by reading Psalm 23. Just because most people are familiar with this, that is no reason for not reading it with a bereaved person. In fact it is probably a very good reason for choosing to read it.

The God of all comfort

The phrase "the God of all comfort" comes in 2 Corinthians 1:3. That verse and the following one are full of instruction. A Christian counselor would benefit from knowing them by heart.

"Praise be to the God and Father of our Lord Jesus Christ, the Father of compassion and the God of all comfort, who comforts us in all our troubles, so that we can comfort those in any trouble with the comfort we ourselves have received from God." *2 Corinthians 1:3, 4*

Unpack these verses

These two verses repay study and reflection.

1. In times of bereavement look to God: "Praise be to the God…"
2. In times of bereavement remember who God is: he is the "Father of our Lord Jesus Christ."
3. In times of bereavement we look to our God who is "the Father of compassion."

4. In times of bereavement we seek comfort from God who is "the God of all comfort."

5. In times of bereavement we know that it is God "who comforts us in all our troubles."

6. In times of bereavement we may not realize what good may come from the time of sadness we are going through. It may be that as a result of all the comfort God gave us during our time of loss "we can comfort those in any trouble with the comfort we ourselves have received from God."

Human comfort

While it is true that we are told not to put our trust in other people, it is also true that God does provide other people to comfort us. While this sounds like a rather obvious truth, the spiritual principle behind it is often forgotten. The great super-apostle Paul, who was more charismatic than any Christians at Corinth, was once greatly comforted "by the coming of Titus" 2 Corinthians 7:6.

So if you are seeking to comfort a bereaved person ensure that he/she has human comfort as well as spiritual comfort.

How to counsel the backslider

A ministry of rebuking

To listen to some Christian preaching you would think that it was a top priority for Christians to go round telling people off and rebuking everybody they meet.

Of course, there is much about rebuking in the Bible.

1. Jesus rebuked Peter and called him "Satan," see Matthew 16:23.
2. Nathan, after his little parable, rounded on King David very directly: 2 Samuel 12:7.
3. Elijah rebuked sinful King Ahab: 1 Kings 21:20.
4. Micaiah also rebuked sinful King Ahab: 1 Kings 22:14.
5. Elisha rebuked King Jehoram: 2 Kings 3:14.
6. Daniel pronounced God's judgment on King Belshazzar: Daniel 5:22.

Helping a backslider

But open rebuke and shouting at the top of your voice is probably never the appropriate approach for a backslider.

There is crystal clear teaching about the "tone of voice" you should have if you are with someone who has seen better days in their Christian life.

When Paul was at his wits' end with all the crazy, non-Christian things the Corinthian Christians were indulging in he tells them, "By the *meekness* and

gentleness of Christ, I *appeal* to you"
2 Corinthians 10:1.

Jude says, "be merciful to those who doubt" Jude 22.

Paul was like a mother

It may not be the general impression we have from reading his letters that Paul was like a mother, a tender, caring parent with his new-born Christians. But this is how he describes himself. Paul reminds the Thessalonians that he and his helpers were *"gentle"* when they were with them: 1 Thessalonians 2:7. This verse ends, "…like a mother caring for her little children."

Paul then goes on to say, "We loved you so much that we were delighted to share with you not only the gospel of God but our lives as well, because you had become so dear to us"
1 Thessalonians 2:8. Paul is gently guiding these new Christians into the right paths. He does not do it by shouting, but by praising them.

God is likened to a mother

At the end of the book of Isaiah, after telling the Israelites how unfaithful they had been to God, Isaiah leaves them with two pictures of the Lord's great love.

1. The Lord is like a nurse with a baby

"For you will nurse and be satisfied at her comforting breasts; you will drink deeply and delight in her overflowing abundance…you will nurse and be

carried on her arm and dandled on her knees." *Isaiah 66:11, 12*

2. The Lord is like a mother

"As a mother comforts her child, so will I comfort you; and you will be comforted over Jerusalem." *Isaiah 66:13*

Bible verses for Christians who have given up on witnessing

The main role of a Christian counselor is not to be judging, telling everyone off, and always taking the moral high ground. No. Christian counselors are just messengers. It is far better for a person to read a few Bible references that you may jot down for them, than for you to condemn them. We all stand or fall before Jesus, not before each other. Here are some helpful Bible verses for anyone who doesn't feel like being a witness for Jesus any more:

- Matthew 10:32, 33
- Romans 10:9, 10
- John 12:42, 43
- Mark 8:38.

Verses for Christians who have stopped reading their Bibles

- 1 Peter 2:2
- Acts 20:32
- James 1:21, 22
- 2 Timothy 3:13-17
- Ephesians 6:17
- Psalm 119:9, 11, 130; 1:1-2
- Joshua 1:8
- Acts 17:11.

More about backsliders

Two types of backslider

Backsliders, who are sometimes referred to as apostates in the Bible, fall into two categories:

- backsliders who want to return to Jesus, and
- backsliders who give no indication of wanting to come back to Jesus.

The art of counseling

It takes great sensitivity and humility to be a helpful counselor to any kind of backslider.

Augustine refers to Christians helping fellow-Christians as an *art*.

"When we are weighed down by poverty, and grief makes us sad; when bodily pain makes us restless, and exile despondent; or when any other grievance afflicts us, if there be good people at hand who understand the art of rejoicing with the joyful and weeping with the sorrowful, who know how to speak a cheerful word and uplift us, then bitterness is mitigated, worries are alleviated and our troubles are overcome."
Augustine of Hippo

We might say that all too often this is a lost art. One of the major reasons that there are so many backsliders is because no sympathetic Christian was to hand to give wise counsel when the person we now label as a "backslider" first felt that they were sinking. All Christians need to be "good people at hand who understand the *art* of rejoicing with the joyful and weeping with the sorrowful, who know how to speak a cheerful word."

Writing to a backslider

What should be written in a letter to a backslider? Sometimes writing a letter to a backslider is a good idea. It might at least convey the idea that someone cares for him/her.

Here's how Basil the Great, 330–379, the founder of the ideal of monastic community life, wrote to a monk who had sinned:

"Be aware of God's compassion, that it heals with oil and wine.
Do not lose hope of salvation.
Remember what is written:
   a. the one who falls shall rise again, and
   b. the one who turns away shall turn again;
   c. the wounded is healed;
   d. the one caught by wild beasts escapes; the one who confesses his sins to God is not rejected.
For the Lord does not want the sinner to die, but to return and live.

There is still
   a. time for endurance,
   b. time for patience,
   c. time for healing,
   d. time for change.
Have you fallen? Rise up.
Have you sinned? Cease.
Do not stand among sinners, but
   keep away from them.
For when you turn back and weep,
   then you will be saved."
   Basil the Great

Backsliders who seem not to want to return

Relevant verses for this sad condition include the following:

- Jeremiah 2:5, 13, 19
- Amos 4:11, 12
- 1 Kings 11:9
- Proverbs 14:14.

Backsliders who indicate that they do want to return

Relevant Bible verses for the above include:

- Jeremiah 3:12, 13, 22; 29:11-13
- Hosea 14:1-4
- Isaiah 43:22, 24, 25; 44:20-22
- Deuteronomy 4:28-31
- 2 Chronicles 7:14; 15:4; 33:12, 13
- 1 John 1:9; 2:1, 2
- Luke 15:11-24.

Loss of our first love

All backsliders will have lost their first love for Jesus.
   In Revelation 2:1-7 a letter to the church in Ephesus accuses some like this: "I hold this against you: You have forsaken your *first love*" Revelation 2:4.
   The remedy for this is given:

- **Remember** the height from which you have fallen: Revelation 2:5.
- **Repent** and do the things you did at first: Revelation 2:5.

Christian counselors are to be living sacrifices

Romans 12:1

"Therefore, I urge you, brothers, in view of God's mercy, to offer your bodies as living sacrifices, holy and pleasing to God–this is your spiritual act of worship" Romans 12:1. To continue to be an effective Christian counselor we must remember that we are in God's service and that all the spiritual principles we may advise other people about should be apparent in our own lives.

Even for the apostle Paul, it was not a matter of: "You listen to me, I've arrived. I have no more to learn." Paul was a great one for learning from other Christians himself. This is how he put it at the beginning of his letter to the Romans: "I long to see you so that I may impart to you some spiritual gift to make you strong–that is, that you and I may be *mutually encouraged* by each other's faith."

Give yourself a spiritual check-up

1. *Our tongues* should be:

   a. speaking up for God: Psalm 107:2
   b. guarded: Proverbs 21:23
   c. bring healing: Proverbs 15:4
   d. gentle: Proverbs 25:15
   e. kept on a tight rein: James 1:26.

2. *Our ears* should be:

   a. hearing: Proverbs 20:12
   b. listening closely: Proverbs 4:20
   c. open to words of knowledge: Proverbs 23:12
   d. listening attentively to the Book of the Law: Nehemiah 8:3.

3. *Our eyes* should be:

   a. good: Matthew 6:22, "If your eyes are good, your whole body will be full of light."
   b. lifted up in God's direction: Psalm 121:1
   c. alert, open, and in focus: Proverbs 20:12
   d. closed to any bribes: Deuteronomy 16:19.

4. *Our feet* should be:

   a. washed by the Lord and made clean: John 13:5-10
   b. wearing the appropriate footwear that comes from the gospel of peace: Ephesians 6:15
   c. steady, because God does not let it slip: Psalm 121:3
   d. beautiful, because they bring good news: Romans 10:15.

5. *Our hands* should be:

a. clean: Psalm 24:3

b. helpful: Ecclesiastes 9:10

c. diligent: Proverbs 12:24

d. rejoicing in everything you put your hand to: Deuteronomy 12:7.

6. *Our minds* should be:

a. renewed: Romans 12:2

b. pure: 2 Peter 3:1

c. concentrating on God: Isaiah 26:3

d. humble: Philippians 2:3.

Being in God's service

We want to grow as Christians in order to bring glory to God. So you can continue with this spiritual check-up and see how you fare with what is demanded in God's service:

1. A transformed life: Romans 12:2.
2. Talents used for his glory: Romans 12:6-8.
3. Sincere love: Romans 12:9.
4. Devotion to fellow-Christians, as you show them brotherly love: Romans 12:10.
5. Never lack zeal: Romans 12:11.
6. Plenty of spiritual fervor: Romans 12:11.
7. Faithful in prayer: Romans 12:12.
8. Hospitable: Romans 12:13.
9. Never conceited: Romans 12:16.
10. At peace with everyone: Romans 12:18.
11. Have love for your enemies: Romans 12:19, 20.
12. Not overcome by evil, but overcoming evil with good: Romans 12:21.

Each member belongs to all the others

Am I my brother's keeper?

This is the cheeky answer Cain gave to the Lord, just after he had murdered his brother Abel. Of course, Christians believe that we are each other's keepers. We have been put in a Christian fellowship so that we can survive and help each other.

Every Christian, every day, like it or not, acts as a Christian counselor. It's not just pastors and ministers, but it's parents, and everybody who works or studies. We all have friends and people we know. Each day we are either an encouragement to our group, or a drag on our group.

Each member belongs to all the others

This is what Paul says in Romans 12:5. What gifts, talents and time we have, we share with our fellow-Christians.

An A to Z check-up

All Christians are meant to be in God's "full time" service, no matter what job or course of study they do. It's a serious business being in God's service. One of the biggest reasons why so many Christians fall by the wayside is that they think that they are okey spiritually speaking, and before they know it they are on a downward track.

See how you get on with the following

a to z of what believers should be like.

a. Christians should be kind to one another: Ephesians 4:32.

b. Christians should honor others above themselves: Romans 12:10.

c. Christians should live in harmony with one another: Romans 12:16.

d. Christians should love one another: Romans 13:8; John 13:34, 35.

e. Christians should build each other up in the Christian faith: Romans 14:19; 1 Thessalonians 5:11.

f. Christians should instruct one another in Christian teaching: Romans 15:14.

g. Christians should bear one another's burdens: Galatians 6:2.

h. Christians should not allow divisions to grow in the fellowship, but have equal concern for each other: 1 Corinthians 12:25.

i. Christians should not lie to each other: Colossians 3:9.

j. Christians should not slander one another: James 4:11.

k. Christians should not grumble against each other: James 5:9.

l. Christians should bear with one another in love: Ephesians 4:2.

m. Christians should be kind and compassionate to one another: Ephesians 4:32.

n. Christians should be forgiving to each other: Ephesians 4:32.

o. Christians should submit to one another out of reverence for Jesus: Ephesians 5:21.

p. Christians should in humility consider others better than themselves: Philippians 2:3.

q. Christians should teach one another and sing hymns with gratitude in their hearts to God: Colossians 3:16.

r. Christians should encourage each other: 1 Thessalonians 4:18.

s. Christians should encourage one another daily: Hebrews 3:13.

t. Christians should consider how to spur one another on towards love and good deeds: Hebrews 10:24.

u. Christians should not give up meeting together: Hebrews 10:25.

v. Christians should confess their sins to each other: James 5:16.

w. Christians should pray for one another: James 5:16; 1 Samuel 12:23.

x. Christians should be sympathetic to one another: 1 Peter 3:8.

y. Christians should offer hospitality to one another without grumbling: 1 Peter 4:9.

z. Christians should serve others with whatever gifts they have: 1 Peter 4:10.

The Counselor

Counseling and the Counselor

No Christian counselor will ever be spiritually effective without the Holy Spirit being at work at the beginning, during, and at the end of all of his/her counseling.

Jesus, just before he left his disciples, spoke at length about the Holy Spirit. Jesus introduced the Holy Spirit to his disciples by referring to him as the "Counselor," John 14–16.

Absent Jesus, present Spirit

Naturally Jesus' disciples were upset to hear Jesus talking about him leaving them. But Jesus told them that although he was going away he would send them "another" Counselor, John 14:16. The Greek word for "another" means "another of the same kind." The Christian counselor must continually seek guidance and teaching from the Holy Spirit, as this is his work today, John 14:26, just as it was Jesus' work when he was physically on this earth.

Counselor

The Greek word for "Counselor" is *parakletos*, meaning one who comes alongside. In all counseling work we should be praying that the Holy Spirit will encourage, comfort and rebuke, as we attempt to counsel in his power. Jesus promised no less than that the Holy Spirit would be with his followers forever, John 14:16, so any Christian attempting to counsel without the living presence of God, may as well give up.

Living after Pentecost

Before Pentecost, see Acts 1:4-5; 2:1-12, the Holy Spirit was active. He often came upon people for specific work at special times, as in the ministry of Elijah the prophet. But, today, for us who live after the coming of the Holy Spirit at

Pentecost, the Holy Spirit can be with us all the time.

Note that the Holy Spirit is the agent of God the Father, and that his ministry in the life of a Christian is to whisper the message of Jesus within us, John 15:26. Anybody claiming to be working under the guidance of the Holy Spirit who does not testify about Jesus is working under false pretenses.

Grieving the Holy Spirit

Each day and each time we engage in any counseling we should ask to be filled by the Holy Spirit and so equipped for the task in hand.

It is, sadly, all too possible to work against the Holy Spirit. Christians do, and can:

- **grieve** the Holy Spirit: Ephesians 4:30; Isaiah 63:10;
- **resist** the Holy Spirit: Acts 7:51;
- **lie** to the Holy Spirit: Acts 5:3;
- **test** the Holy Spirit: Acts 5:9.

The ministry of the Holy Spirit

Christian counselors need to be aware of the ministry of the Holy Spirit and constantly seek help from him. Note the different aspects of his work.

1. The Holy Spirit testifies about Jesus: John 15:26.
2. The Holy Spirit brings glory to Jesus: John 16:14.
3. The Holy Spirit guides into the truth: John 16:13.
4. The Holy Spirit convicts the world

of guilt: John 16:7-11.
5. The Holy Spirit gives spiritual life: John 6:63.
6. The Holy Spirit lives in believers: John 14:16.
7. The Holy Spirit teaches all things: John 14:26.
8. The Holy Spirit is a deposit guaranteeing our inheritance: Ephesians 1:13, 14.
9. The Holy Spirit pours out God's love in the hearts of Christians: Romans 5:3-5.
10. The Holy Spirit searches the deep things of God: 1 Corinthians 2:10.
11. The Holy Spirit fills the believer: Ephesians 5:18.
12. The Holy Spirit moves believers to follow his decrees: Ezekiel 36:27.
13. The Holy Spirit brings encouragement to churches: Acts 9:31.
14. The Holy Spirit helps us in our weakness: Romans 8:26.
15. The Holy Spirit intercedes for Christians: Romans 8:26, 27.
16. The Holy Spirit makes Christians overflow with hope: Romans 15:13; Galatians 5:5.
17. The Holy Spirit gives power to Christians to witness: Luke 24:46-49; Acts 1:8.
18. The Holy Spirit brings spiritual strength to churches: Acts 9:31.
19. The Holy Spirit calls Christians to be pastors: Acts 20:28.
20. The Holy Spirit calls Christians to be missionaries: Acts 13:2.

Watch out for false teachers and false prophets

Paul the pastor

Paul spent a great deal of time warning against false teachers. As a pastor he felt that it was he duty to warn God's flock against the wolves who appeared in sheep's clothing in so many of the early churches: Acts 20:29.

Identify the enemy

Christian counselors need to know their spiritual enemy. Here are some of the characteristics of false prophets and false teachers.

1. They are Satan's servants
   "For such men are false apostles, deceitful workmen, masquerading as apostles of Christ. And no wonder, for Satan himself masquerades as an angel of light. It is not surprising, then, if his servants masquerade as servants of righteousness. Their end will be what their actions deserve" 2 Corinthians 11:13-15.
2. Moses warned against false prophets: Deuteronomy 13:1-5; 18:20-22.
3. False prophets often appear to be in the majority. Elijah had to battle against 850 false prophets: 1 Kings 18:17-19.
4. False prophets often have top positions in the ranks of the "official" ecclesiastical hierarchy. Jesus was constantly crossing swords with the Pharisees: Matthew 23:1-36.
5. Paul's ministry was sometimes put in jeopardy from false Christians:

2 Corinthians 11:26.
6. Paul warned pastor Titus, who was shepherding God's flock on the Mediterranean island of Crete, to be on the lookout for deceivers: Titus 1:10.
7. Peter sent out warnings about false teachers in his second letter: 2 Peter 2:1.
8. John, at length, warns about false prophets and the spirit of anti-Christ in the same breath, telling his readers not to believe every spirit, but to test the spirits.

"Dear friends, do not believe every spirit, but test the spirits to see whether they are from God, because many false prophets have gone out into the world. This is how you can recognize the Spirit of God: Every spirit that acknowledges that Jesus Christ has come in the flesh is from God, but every spirit that does not acknowledge Jesus is not from God. This is the spirit of the antichrist, which you have heard is coming and even now is already in the world." *1 John 4:1-3*

The message pedaled by false teachers

1. False teachers preach another gospel: Galatians 1:8, 9; Matthew 7:21-23.
2. False teachers change the grace of God into:
   - a license for immorality and
   - deny that Jesus Christ is our only Sovereign and Lord: Jude 4.

Oppose false teaching

One of the characteristics that should mark out overseers, according to Paul comes in Titus 1:9.

An overseer/elder must:

1. be faithful to the message of the Christian gospel. "He must hold firmly to the trustworthy message as it has been taught."
2. teach this message. "...so that he can encourage others by sound doctrine."
3. be able to counter false teaching. "...refute those who oppose it [sound doctrine]."

Learn how to teach the true gospel

Paul's answer to false teachers was very simple. Christian pastors were to teach the truth.

There are many hints about how to speak effectively for Jesus in the Bible:

1. Ask God for help as you start to prepare: Psalm 119:18.
2. Choose a Bible text to base your message on: Luke 4:17-19.
3. Meditate on God's Word: Joshua 1:8.
4. Compare scripture with scripture. Make the Bible the yardstick with which every other idea is compared: Acts 17:11. The Bereans examined the Scriptures daily.
5. Make sure that Jesus is the center of your message: Luke 24:27; Acts 8:35.
6. Collect illustrations to shed light on God's eternal truths: Matthew 13:34.
7. Don't forever remain a timid Timothy. Preach: 2 Timothy 4:2.

What about the weak?

Help the weak

Just as Jesus said that we should help to feed the hungry, and clothe the naked, Matthew 25:35, so Paul wrote that "we must help the weak," Acts 20:35.

The weak in faith

Some people seem to have very weak faith all the time. This requires action. All too often the weak in faith are left on the sidelines and never asked to join in any Christian form of service.

Our duty to the weak in faith is clearly stated in Romans 14:1.

1. Accept the weak in faith.
2. Do not pass judgment on disputable matters with the weak in faith.

3. Do not look down on the weak in faith or despise his beliefs and practices.
4. Remember, God has accepted the weak in faith: Read Romans 14:1-4.
5. We who are strong should bear with the failings of the weak. Strong Christians are told that they should not just tolerate weak Christians. Rather they should help them and affirm them in a loving way. Paul goes on to say that strong Christians should not ride roughshod over the scruples of weak Christians, and so live a life pleasing themselves. Romans 15:1, 2.
6. Some people have weak consciences. Paul says that to the weak he became weak. If it meant upsetting a fellow-Christian, Paul was quite happy to forego the Christian freedom he had about eating meat which had been sacrificed to idols. It is the responsibility of the strong to give way to the weak:
1 Corinthians 9:22.
7. Do not be a stumbling-block to the weak, writes Paul:
1 Corinthians 8:9-13.
8. Help the weak. It is very interesting to note that in 1 Thessalonians 5:14 Paul lays down what our attitude should be to different people. The idle, for example, should be warned. But it is a different matter when it comes to the weak.
   • The weak are to helped.

- The timid are to be encouraged.
- Strong Christians are to be patient with everyone.

Bible verses for the weak

One practical way to help the weak is to be forever encouraging them to stick with God's great promises which were made specifically for weak people, although, of course, they can be used by everyone.

1. God knows about our frailties: Psalm 78:39.
2. God is like a caring father and has compassion on us: Psalm 103:13.
3. In our distress God lifts us up: Isaiah 63:9.
4. Jesus is our high priest and is more than able to sympathize with our weaknesses: Hebrews 4:15.

Practical action on behalf of the weak

1. Share what you have

"Is it not to share your food with the hungry and to provide the poor wanderer with shelter–when you see the naked to clothe him, and not to turn away from your own flesh and blood?" *Isaiah 58:7*

2. Be helpful to the weak

"In everything I did, I showed you that by this kind of hard work we must help the weak, remembering the words the Lord Jesus himself said: 'It is more blessed to give than to receive.'" *Acts 20:35*

3. Be a burden-bearer

"Carry each other's burdens, and in this way you will fulfil the law of Christ." *Galatians 6:2*

4. Show practical concern to those who have fallen and to the abused

"Remember those in prison as if you were their fellow prisoners, and those who are mistreated as if you yourselves were suffering." *Hebrews 13:3*

5. Care for the needy

"Religion that God our Father accepts as pure and faultless is this: to look after the orphans and widows in their distress and to keep oneself from being polluted by the world." *James 1:27*

What about the wanderers?

The wanderers

"My brothers, if one of you should wander from the truth and someone should bring him back, remember this: Whoever turns a sinner from the error of his way will save him from death and cover over a multitude of sins."
James 5:19

Sinning Christians need to be restored. When we wander from the truth we need someone to lead us back into God's ways.

The right word

Christian counselors need to pray that they will say the right word every time they are trying to help a fellow-Christian.

Here, an important verse to meditate on is Isaiah 50:4: "The Sovereign Lord has given me an instructed tongue, to know the word that sustains the weary."

Have you ever prayed for "an instructed tongue"?

Have you ever prayed to have just the right word that will sustain the depressed?

The very words of God

Christian counseling is a high calling, and a great responsibility. The choice of words used in counseling is crucial. Peter wrote: "If anyone speaks, he should do it as one speaking the very words of God" 1 Peter 4:11. In Greek the words "very words" refer to the Scriptures and to the words God has spoken. Christian counselors need to base what they say on

the Bible. There are few instances when speaking the "very words of God" (provided that they are appropriate ones) should be withheld.

Reasons for wandering away

There are endless reasons why some Christians wander off from the Christian fellowship and cool down in their love for Jesus.

Whatever these are it's up to the Christian counselor to help that person, not to gossip about them or shake one's head in disapproval or despair.

1. For Christians who no longer pray

None of us feel that our prayer lives could not be improved. So we can but be humble when tackling this subject.

Helpful verses about the importance of prayer are:

- James 4:2; 5:13-18
- Luke 1:9-13; 6:12; 22:9-13
- Isaiah 40:31
- Psalm 55:17
- Daniel 6:10
- 1 Thessalonians 5:17.

The dangers of prayerlessness are:

a. It is a hallmark of evildoers: Psalm 53:4
b. It is something that God hates: see Isaiah 43:22
c. It may bring disaster: Daniel 9:13
d. It is linked with turning our back on God: Zephaniah 1:6.

2. For Christians who now live careless lives

When Christians stop going to church or stop attending prayer meetings and Bible studies it is quite a step for them to come back. For many such people feel that everybody will be looking at them, and even condemning them. All Christians need to put themselves out in being really friendly towards any who come back after a time away from Christian fellowship.

Helpful Bible verses for Christians who have been living careless lives are:

- 2 Corinthians 6:14–7:1
- Matthew 6:24
- 1 John 2:15-17

- James 4:4, 6-8
- Hebrews 12:14
- 1 Peter 1:13-19; 4:17, 18
- Luke 8:14; 21:34-36; 12:35-38
- Romans 12:1, 2; 14:23
- 2 Timothy 4:7, 8.

The dangers of spiritual indifference are:

a. Spiritual indifference may lead to arrogance: Psalm 123:4.
b. Spiritual indifference may lead to complacency: Isaiah 32:9.
c. Spiritual indifference may lead to a sense of false security: Zephaniah 1:12.
d. Spiritual indifference will lead to the loss of one's first love for Jesus: Matthew 24:12.

What about false shepherds?

5. False shepherds lead the sheep astray: Jeremiah 50:6.
6. False shepherds only care for themselves: Ezekiel 34:2.
7. False shepherds feed and clothe themselves, but take no care of the flock: Ezekiel 34:3.
8. False shepherds run away when a wolf is about to attack the flock: John 10:12.

Many people would, humanly speaking, still be active Christians if they had been protected from false shepherds. The other way for Christians to survive this onslaught of evil false shepherds is for Christians to become mature in their faith and understanding of the Christian life.

Unfaithful ministers

Unfaithful ministers have always existed. While it may appear that high profile scandals connected with some well-known tele-evangelists do great harm to the reputation of Christians, the Christian church has always survived these dreadful happenings.

Unfaithful ministers mentioned in the Bible

- Isaiah 56:10
- Jeremiah 6:13; 23:11
- Lamentations 2:14
- Ezekiel 33:6
- Micah 3:11
- "It is true that some preach Christ out of envy and rivalry" Philippians 1:15.

False shepherds

As well as false teachers the Bible warns against false shepherds. These are the people who should be faithful pastors but are not. It is vital who spot false shepherds as Christians seem to have a weakness about following these charlatans.

Characteristics of false shepherds:

1. False shepherds love to sleep: Isaiah 56:10.
2. False shepherds lack understanding: Isaiah 56:11.
3. False shepherds encourage drunkenness: Isaiah 56:12.
4. False shepherds scatter the flock: Jeremiah 23:2.

Examples of neglecting God's service include:

1. The Gadites and Reubenites who did not want to go to war: Numbers 32:6.
2. Joshua had to rebuke the Israelites for not taking possession of the Promised Land: Joshua 18:3.
3. The angel of the Lord cursed the people of Meroz because they did not come to the help of the Lord: Judges 5:23.
4. The men of Tekoa did not put their shoulders to the work of rebuilding the wall of Jerusalem: Nehemiah 3:5.
5. Jeremiah went so far as to say that a curse would be put on people who did not do the Lord's work: Jeremiah 48:10.
6. James asked a rhetorical question about what good could it do anyone who claimed to have faith but had no deeds? James 2:14.
7. James went on to say that it was a sin if you knew what you should do and did not do it. James 4:17.
8. The man who is deaf to the cries of the poor will find that his own cries for help will not be heard: Proverbs 21:13.
9. Ezekiel tells of the uncaring shepherds who did not strengthen the weak, heal the sick, or bandage up the wounds of the injured. He also rebuked them for not searching for the stray sheep and for not bringing back the lost: Ezekiel 34:4.

Supporting Christians under fire

Persecution

Persecution of Christians is nothing new. It has been claimed that there were more Christians martyred in the twentieth century than in all the previous centuries put together. However, most Christians in the West remain ignorant of such terrible treatment of their fellow-believers.

Using protests

Today, in an attempt to help imprisoned Christians some Christians have used all the methods of protest which are legitimately open to them.

Certainly Paul did not ignore the laws of the land, and he made use of them when he could.

Paul imprisoned at Philippi

It was illegal for Roman citizens to be beaten in public. Paul and Silas had undergone this without even a trial. Paul rebuked the authorities by telling them that he was a Roman citizen. Read Acts 16:16-40, especially verse 37.

Paul used his Roman citizenship to good advantage on another occasion which is also recorded in Acts. See Acts 22:22-29.

Using prayer

The early church used prayer as its main response to persecution. On the orders of King Herod, James, the brother of John, had just been beheaded. See Acts 12:2. Peter had been imprisoned by

King Herod. The night before Herod had intended to put Peter on trial Peter was miraculously rescued by an angel from prison. See Acts 12:6-19.

But the key verse here is Acts 12:5: "So Peter was kept in prison, but the church was earnestly praying to God for him."

So, today, we should act in the same way, when faced with persecution, or when we have to support fellow-Christians who are persecuted. We should use every lawful means possible to secure their safety. And we should never neglect prayer.

Christians and persecution
The following Bible verses apply to Christians who are going through the fires of persecution:

- 1 Peter 1:4-7; 2:21, 23; 3:17-18; 4:12-14
- Matthew 5:10-12
- 2 Timothy 2:12; 3:12
- Acts 14:22; 5:40-42
- Hebrews 12:1-4
- Revelation 2:10
- Luke 12:32
- Psalm 23:4; 27:1-6, 13-14; 34:17, 19; 46:1-3; 50:15.

The Christian counselor
Faced with persecution, Christians must seek to minister to both the persecuted and to the loved ones of the persecuted, as well as to the Christian fellowship from which the persecuted comes.

This applies to any trial Christians may be called to undergo. A great

number of different kinds of attacks against God's followers are recorded in the Bible. We need to be alert to them and react to them in a Christian way.

Trials which test a Christian's faith
Trials which face Christians comes in all shapes and sizes. Such trials include:

1. Temptation to commit adultery: see Joseph in Genesis 39:7-20
2. Ridicule: see Nehemiah in Nehemiah 2:18-20; 4:1; 6:15
3. Hatred: see Haman's hatred towards Mordecai: Esther 3:1-5; 10:1-3
4. Satan: see Job in Job 1:12–2:10; see also Ananias in Acts 5:3
5. Public persecution: see Jeremiah in Jeremiah 1:19; 20:2; 38:6
6. Prejudice in the hearts of God's followers: see Jonah in Jonah 3:10–4:11
7. The laws of the land: See Daniel's three friends in Daniel 3:1-25
8. False accusations: see Daniel in Daniel 6:3-24
9. False religions: see Elijah in 1 Kings 16:30–18:46
10. Love of money: see Judas in Matthew 26:14-16
11. Worldly possessions: see the rich young man who came to Jesus in Matthew 19:16-22
12. Ego: see Peter in Matthew 26:33, 34, 69-75
13. Love of the world: see Demas in 2 Timothy 4:10. Demas "deserted" because he loved the world.

Counseling in a crisis

The death of a baby

"I everywhere teach that no one can
be justly condemned and perish
except on account of actual sin; and to
say that the countless mortals taken
from life while yet infants are
precipitated from their mother's arms
into eternal death is a blasphemy to be
universally detested." *John Calvin*

The death of a child

Luther's bereavement

"My little daughter Elizabeth is dead.
She has left me wonderfully sick at
heart and almost womanish. I am so
moved by pity for her. I could never
have believed a father's heart could be
so tender for his child. Pray to God for
me." *Martin Luther*

Mrs R. A. Torrey

"I'm so glad Elizabeth is with the
Lord, and not in that box." *Mrs R. A.
Torrey, at the funeral of her 12-year-old
daughter*

On the death of a husband or wife

"It is a slight consolation to tell you
that I sympathize deeply with your
grief, but this is all human friends can
do for you, as you have to turn to God
for everything else. And indeed,
Madame, I do turn with my whole

heart to the Comforter of the afflicted
and the strength of the weak.
  I do not pray that God will take
away your grief but that he will
transform it so that you may benefit
from it, and so, not overwhelm you.
When God parts two people, who
have been united in the most sacred
bonds, he is sending a blessing on
them both. God takes the first person
into his own eternal glory, and
through his healing sorrow he saves
the second person who is left for a
short time in this world."
François Fènelon, Letters

The hope of heaven

"I tell you the truth, he who believes
  has everlasting life." *John 6:47*

Accept sorrow

"Ah, if you knew what peace there is
in an accepted sorrow!" *Madam Guyon,
A Short and Easy Method of Prayer*

Revelation's picture of heaven

"Then I saw a new heaven and a new
earth, for the first heaven and the
first earth had passed away, and
there was no longer any sea. I saw
the Holy City, the new Jerusalem,
coming down out of heaven from
God, prepared as a bride beautifully

dressed for her husband. And I heard a loud voice from the throne saying, 'Now the dwelling of God is with men, and he will live with them. They will be his people, and God himself will be with them and be their God.

No more tears

"'He will wipe every tear from their eyes. There will be no more death or mourning or crying or pain, for the old order of things has passed away.'

Everything new

"He who was seated on the throne said, 'I am making everything new!' Then he said, 'Write this down, for these words are trustworthy and true.'

The Alpha and the Omega

"He said to me: 'It is done. I am the Alpha and the Omega, the Beginning and the End. To him who is thirsty I will give to drink without cost from the spring of the water of life. He who overcomes will inherit all this, and I will be his God and he will be my son.'" *Revelation 21:1-7*

The beatific vision

"We shall rest and we shall see, we shall see and we shall love, we shall love and we shall praise. Behold what shall be in the end without end. For what else is our end except to reach the kingdom which has no end?" *Augustine, The City of God*

Days of grief

"Your days of grief will come to an end. I, the Lord, will be your eternal light, more lasting than the sun and moon." *Isaiah 60:20, GNB*

Keep growing, Christian counselor

Never forget the devil

Satan never goes to sleep. His evil mission is to make all Christians ineffective. He does that by every direct and indirect attack you can think of. His three main methods are:

1. through false teaching
2. through persecution
3. through making individual Christians doubt their salvation.

Two truths to remember

1. The whole world is under the control of the evil one: 1 John 5:19.
2. "In this world you will have trouble. But take heart! I have overcome the world" John 16:33.

Grow, grow, grow

We follow in Jesus' footsteps, 1 Peter 2:21, when we:

B – Believe in Jesus: John 1:12.
Y – Yield our lives to Jesus: Romans 12:1.

G – Go to God in prayer: 1 John 5:14, 15.
R – Read and study God's word: Revelation 1:3; 2 Timothy 2:15.
O – Obey his commands: John 15:14.
W – Witness to Jesus: Luke 8:39.
I – Ignore the deeds of darkness: Ephesians 5:11.
N – Never hold anything back for God: 1 Thessalonians 5:19.
G – Give God your talents and your money: Matthew 25:20; 2 Corinthians 9:7.

I – Increase your fruitfulness: John 15:8.
N – Neglect not God's gift in you: 1 Timothy 4:14; 2 Timothy 1:6.

G – Go to church: Hebrews 10:25.
R – Redeem the time: Ephesians 5:16; 2 Timothy 2:4.
A – Avoid every kind of evil: 1 Thessalonians 5:22.
C – Conquer Satan and his temptations: James 4:7; Matthew 26:41.
E – Expect Jesus' return: Hebrews 9:28.